To Donna —
Enjoy
Frances King
April, '91

A WESTERN HARVEST

THE GATHERINGS OF AN EDITOR

SELECTED AND INTRODUCED BY
FRANCES RING

John Daniel and Company
SANTA BARBARA · 1991

Typography by Jim Cook
Cover design by Francine Rudesill

PHOTO CREDITS: Lawrence Clark Powell (page 14) by John P. Schaefer; Anaïs
Nin (page 45) by Robert A. Fitzgerald, Jr.; Wallace Stegner (page 54) by Leo Holub;
M.F.K. Fisher (page 109) by George T. Krusf; William Saroyan (page 138) by
William Childress; Davis Dutton (page 160) by Marc Brian.

Published by John Daniel and Company, Publishers
Post Office Box 21922, Santa Barbara, California 93121

LIBRARY OF CONGRESS CATALOGING-IN-PUBLICATION DATA
A Western harvest: the gatherings of an editor / selected and
introduced by Frances Ring.
    Profiles by Frances Ring include correspondence.
    p.   cm.
    ISBN 0-936784-87-3
    1. California—Civilization.   2. Southwest, New—Civilization.
I. Ring, Frances Kroll.
F861.W46   1991   90-13882
979.4—dc 20   CIP

For L.C.P.

Contents

A WESTERN HARVEST

To Begin With . . .

AS FAR BACK as I can remember—and it is a tattered ribbon of time—I have played with words. Oh, I had my share of child's play, but no memory compares to the marvel of receiving my first big, royal-blue book of fairy tales with the golden hair of Rapunzel sprayed over the cover. I was four years old and moved readily into storyland. I sat spellbound as I was read to until I learned to read. Eventually, I was introduced to the public library where I could borrow six books at a time and hurry to finish them so I could borrow more.

This was, of course, a pre-television era. Radio and movies were doled-out treats. Reading was our entertainment, adventure, fantasy, and romance. In time, I fell wildly in love with Rochester, Martin Eden, Dr. Arrowsmith. I played Rebecca in a class reading of *Ivanhoe*. I wandered through the forest primeval in quest of poetic ecstasy. And just the sight of a romantic couple holding hands in the park would hurry me home to set down love ballads, since lost to posterity.

The hours I spent with Jane Austen, George Eliot, Charles Dickens immersed in the images of other times gave way to the dark realism of Upton Sinclair, Frank Norris, Theodore Dreiser,

7

and John Steinbeck. The social ills of the world were upon us, and in the late thirties my family moved from New York to Los Angeles, where the sun beamed a brighter future. Not only did I turn my attention to the literature of the West, but I became aware of the Europeans who had escaped to Hollywood from their troubled continent in search of temporary peace—Thomas Mann, Aldous Huxley, Christopher Isherwood. Name dropping? No. It's just that the reading habit determined what eventually became my chief interests—writing and editing.

I learned to type and take shorthand and hoped one day to work for a writer. Quite by accident, I landed a job with F. Scott Fitzgerald, who was doing a film stint for the money and working on his last novel. I have written about that experience and mention it here only to point out that my association with this superb craftsman taught me to respect the effort that goes into creative writing, to understand how difficult it is to get it right, and to learn something about editing through observing how aggressively Fitzgerald revised his own work.

Learning to edit. How does one learn it? For me, editing grows out of a respect for writing, out of a feeling that what is written on the page is expressed in the best possible use of language to illuminate an idea or a character or a plot. Editing is something we do all our lives. It's a matter of choice, of selection and discard, and of taste. In retrospect, all my jobs contained an aspect of editing. Story analysis for a motion picture studio involved extracting the essence of a story line, picking out what was vital for the visual impact of a film script, and writing a succinct, dramatic summary of the story. Another area of employment was tape editing of discussions of literature, politics, and sociological problems. To trim these discussions to tapes of half-hour or hour-long recordings meant cutting out excess verbiage so that the speaker sounded lucid and literate—no hesitant sounds or digressions. Book reviewing, too, was a form of editing a story or theme, whether fiction or not, and reducing it to its core for evaluating the content, style, and execution.

There is literal editing in the manner of the word that can be learned at school—line editing, copy editing, correcting spelling, names, dates, word usage, detailing a piece of writing, using appropriate style hieroglyphics. All necessary tasks. And there are people who are very good at them. But my interest is in the presentation of an idea, the concept, the way a subject is translated to the reader; an idea that not only captures the moment but remains with the reader beyond the moment. I like to think of it as creative editing.

In the 1970s, I became editor of *Westways,* a regional publication. California was bursting with cultural growth. It was a scene to be recorded from a historic as well as a contemporary view. California was a haven for writers, artists, and photographers. They were experimental and reflective. They captured the spirit of the Western frontier. Yes, California was and still is a frontier open to an influx of culture carriers from all the world. I had hoped to reflect that movement in our pages.

An editor quickly learns, however, that it is not always possible to break through the barriers of formula. There are the money men or publishers or advertising people who rigidly opt for the tried and true embellished with a bit of glitz. Corporate and creative people have rarely been without conflict. Nonetheless. . . .

I did not go plunging into change. I did try to expand a format that had an established audience for Western history and travel set in motion by previous editors who had left their laudable and individual stamp on the publication for over sixty years. Seated on the other side of the desk from the writer, I had now to put my esteem for the word-players in perspective in order to select material appropriate for the magazine and to reject material that was unsuitable without offending the author's sensibility. How would I say "No, thank you, and good luck in placing it elsewhere"? And if I should get a submission that might require changes from a writer of reputation, how would I deal with that? Would I dare suggest revisions to someone like William Saroyan? Or would I walk a tightrope? Would I be able to deal with temperament? How to deal with prima donnas?

What a relief it was to find that the more established the writer, the more professional the behavior. Almost always, articles carried out the original idea. If small revisions or cuts were necessary, the author was consulted. Some preferred to make their own revisions. Others trusted us because it was my editorial policy not to tamper with the writer's style. Editing had to be scrupulous, mindful of the content and the flow of a sentence. The sharp blue pencil was not for stabbing. I bought a story because I liked it, not because I wanted to turn it into something else. If there were problems with the work—e.g. twice too long, confusing in its development, not well organized—they were resolved before purchase. Why would we consider such a piece at all? Most likely because the idea was good, even unusual. There were times when the writer wanted help in editing, felt too close to the material to make the changes. We would then discuss areas that might be revised or clarified or omitted without excising the author's pet phrase, forever losing it to the waste basket. I neither imposed my style nor did our associates impose their style on a given piece of work. Grammar, syntax, spelling, name-and-date checks went by the manual. All else kept faith with the tone and quality of the manuscript. We served the author while mindful of our own needs and standards.

Certainly, editing a nonfiction magazine is different from editing a novel. There is a creative level to the novel that belongs solely to the writer. The editor may question but not intrude upon the writer's vision. When the right question is asked, it can dissolve or resolve a dilemma or problem for the novelist, who can then rewrite or continue on. But essentially the work belongs to the novelist, whose individual talent differentiates him or her from another writer. There are some who have no desire to share their work with an editor until it is completed, whose ideas are so internalized that they can't or won't talk about them. Others, more gregarious, find it helpful to bounce off ideas, and the difference in the tone of their work often reflects a difference in personality and style.

In editing a magazine, however, the idea and formulation is the editor's creation. Gathering the talent to carry out the concept is the way the editor brings the idea to fruition, and at the same time showcases the separate gifts of the contributors.

Some of the most stimulating material we worked up in the 1970s dealt with California's ethnic population. These assorted peoples settled in our midst with all their colors and problems. We designed certain issues around the new and old citizens. Writers delved into personal history, adjustments to a new land, acceptance into the community, contributions to the culture of the land and the generational progress or lack of it in becoming Californians. We dressed these issues in the costumes and art of the exotic people, many of whom clung to their origins and created their own familiar neighborhood environments to help them adapt to an area which, in many ways, was wary of their integration.

It was of equal interest to unearth, during the planning for the nation's bicentennial in 1976, the original founding families of Los Angeles and to discover a far different mix from our eastern brethren. We asked our regional historians to inform us on the combination of *Mestizos, Indios, Mulatos, Chinos,* and *Españoles* who settled the land. Intermarriage was common then, leaving little purity of race. This multifaced population continues to dominate the city today and to embellish, redesign, complicate, and enrich its human texture.

We posed our heritage alongside the contemporary scene, as Los Angeles was growing so fast it often lost sight of its beginnings. I say *we* because it took a lively, cooperative staff to carry each issue to press. They were talented, were given space to express their individuality, both in writing and in art. We strove for an identifiable look and we had one. We aimed to season each issue with a new flavor while retaining the familiar represented in the regular columns on books, films, media, music, nature, stage, dining. Our personal editorial rapport was ideal for working toward our desire to put out a literate, entertaining publication that reflected the region—until management decided we were going too far afield from the conservative course.

In today's publishing arena, surveys, demographics, and polls are the controls in guiding tastes of readers, just as they are in creating material for viewers of other media. Creative expression is determined by a sales force. Individuality gives way to imitation of what appears to be successful.

A survey is supposedly an indicator of what the people want, but is too often loosely interpreted and manipulated to reflect what the surveyors or publishers want. Fearful of shaking the reader off the couch, the staple diet goes on uninterrupted. Actually, current advertising graphics have gone much farther apace than the editorial content, seducing the audience with visuals and reflecting the dominant influence of television and films on the ". . . worth a thousand words" adage.

Yet, new magazines are being published in great numbers. There is a magazine for everything under the sun—from running to meditation, from animals to Zen. Despite their specialization and the hype that claims to offer something NEW, they, too, play host to fads. The shift to service-oriented publications insidiously affects the general-interest, quality magazines and leaves them teetering on a precarious financial wire until they topple into the arms of a takeover.

Who is to blame? Indications are that it is a trend of the times. Hype and technology produce their own restraints and new norms. Perhaps commercialism has always been inhibiting, but once upon a time, magazines featured short stories every week and serialized novels that were illustrated by fine artists. They were the marketplaces for established talent and opened doors to new talent. I do not cling to the good old days, but I view with sadness the demise of the standard bearers.

An editor keeps on reading piles of manuscripts. Suddenly it's sit-up time. A thrust of language, an idea that travels an adventurous offroad. The awareness of an ingenious newcomer is a shot in the arm. This is one addiction I never want to overcome. I view with pleasure the recognition and encouragement of those young writers who have since gone on to become novelists, biographers, journalists, television producers, and editors. How pleased I am that they kept me from falling asleep on the job.

If there is a message in this to aspiring scribes, it is this: if you have to detour to make a living at a form you're not in love with, don't abandon your style. There is a lot of language to play with. Write your own tune. Even if some editor tampers with your work, something of you remains. Words and the way they are assembled in the larger design are your personal instrument, just as a voice is to a singer. Sing your song. There will be an editor who will hear it and who will print it.

I look back on editing a publication as an embryonic development. Envisioning an issue, conceiving it, seeing it all come together made it my baby, even if there were occasional birth defects. The nurturing of new writers who needed encouragement, of established writers who never grew too old to need praise. Writing is a lonesome task. Someone has to read you and tell you that your work is worth the effort, or let you down without sending a message of despair. And finding a gem in the slushpile may, by a stretch, compare to rescuing an abandoned child.

The writers represented in the following pages all had reputations without my help, but luring them into my fold was a challenge. We exchanged correspondence that was warm and informal, proving that the pen or word-processor and its product could get along with the blue pencil. There were half-serious jokes about money; some nitpicking; the complaint about the occasional, unforgivable typos. Salutations coined nicknames. Signatures were signed with love and other expressions of social endearment that encouraged me to answer in the same tone. Perhaps dealing with a woman editor who wore a soft glove was different from dealing with a male editor over a couple of drinks or lunch. Whatever the reasons, valued friendships ensued.

There were many other writers not included in this limited group—too many to list—whose creativity helped make my task easier. For the pleasure of their professional company, I thank them, wherever they are. That time of my life was something of a good thing.

LAWRENCE CLARK POWELL

LAWRENCE CLARK POWELL

LAWRENCE CLARK POWELL had been writing for *Westways* for some thirty-odd years when I came on staff in 1970. I was assigned to edit his monthly series, "California Classics," followed by "Southwest Classics"—studies of California and Southwest writers and their works. When this series was finished, it coincided with his retirement from UCLA. He was planning to move to Tucson, Arizona. He said he was burned out and couldn't write anymore. We refused to accept his decision.

I drove out to Malibu where he and his wife Fay were packing to leave. The object was to persuade him that he could continue to write for us very easily. All he had to do was to send us a letter from the Southwest. This was new territory for him. He could explore it at leisure and record his impressions. No preparatory reading, no research, just observations and a little travel. He promised nothing. But Powell could no more stop reading and writing than he could stop breathing. At least he had no readiness for a sedentary life. He was the sperm that had fused with the literary egg of Los Angeles and created a colony of book people. Now he would turn his efforts to Arizona.

He became affiliated with the University of Arizona. He helped them build a new library, as he had done at UCLA. He unearthed the drama of the desert, its rivers, and its people. He befriended Southwest culture. Before long, he had enough essays to fill a book. And when his Malibu home (which he had rented) was lost to flames in a tragic coastal fire, he became an official citizen of Tucson. But old ties do not burn. The Powell Library at UCLA will always stand in his honor.

Our friendship aged well over the years. He was a constant correspondent, amusing, bantering, straightforward. When I asked him to do an article on Alan Swallow, one of the early "little" publishers, he sent a postcard:

> May, 1975: Francesca Mia! No can Swallow Alan. Just can't get up any steam. . . . Will see you in June and hopefully plot something else. Will call from Malibu. L.

Or:

> Tucson, June 6, 1975
> Mi Cara Francescita! Check and July issue here in the same mail. I cashed the magazine and read the check muy pronto. And I thank you . . . Love, Larry.

Powell was devoted to fine printing. One of his essays was on Saul and Lillian Marks and their Plantin Press in Los Angeles. Their work was exquisite and their small books became art pieces. I wrote Powell a note of praise. He replied, July 20, 1975:

> Dear Frances, Cara Francesca, hey pal. I'm glad you like the piece on Saul. If you defer payment beyond 30 days, kindly add interest. . . . Flew to SF and then by car to Monterey. Had a great visit with Gordon Newell, Ansel Adams, and Wynn Bullock. Came home the same way. . . . Will be in Santa Fe, Flagstaff July 29-Aug. 3. . . . Will write West to Big Sur, or, the True End of the World. Need a few days to precipitate my essences. Am really filled to the brim. Love, Larry.

In May of 1978, we made one of our rare but good-sized booboos. He responded with his usual wit:

Am so fond of my own prose that it gave me pleasure to read the same paragraph twice!

He was too busy to let a typo bother him, and the rest of his letter was concerned with his activity.

Had nearly 2 hours with Bruce Babbitt, throwing the rest of his schedule into confusion. A very rich session indeed. He sez I have mentored him the way Dobie did me. Will be working on a piece. Am heading north now and will see the family archives. . . . Will keep in touch. . . . Larry.

He could also be generous with praise and write:

There's a certain charm about the August issue even though I ain't therein! Really a lovely issue, particularly F.R. on Nin and Paris. . . .

How could I not resist the stroke? By 1980, he was still feigning retirement and in May of that year he wrote.

Francesca de Ringini, hail! When you want another in yr. Women of the West series, I might do Peggy Pond Church of Santa Fe. You surely know her "The House at Otowi Bridge." I had a bit on her in my Santa Fe piece a couple of months ago. Will be in Santa Fe for opera this summer and I could wrap it up then. OK? Lorenzo.

On his occasional short visits to Los Angeles, we would have lunch. He talked about a possible book on his father, whose contribution to the orange-growing industry and friendship with Herbert Hoover had a place in history. He also wanted to write about the estrangement between his parents during that period, but despite the many years that had passed, it was still difficult for him to deal with it. He put the idea on the burner and ultimately it simmered into a book, *Portrait of My Father*.

Another time he brought Noel Young, the Santa Barbara publisher, to lunch. After a lively meal, Larry sat down at the piano and knocked out old jazz tunes with as much rhythm as if he were in his twenties.

A round of applause is due him for his spirit, intellect, and energy. For me, Powell is a never-aging genie. I'm sure that long after he's gone, he will continue to appear—not out of a bottle, but certainly out of a book.

■

Letter from the Southwest

A drive through the heat and history
of the desert leads to Malibu
where the seaside chill
warms to the presence of old friends

LAWRENCE CLARK POWELL

Now that Frank Dobie, Will Robinson and Ed Ainsworth have all been carried over the river by the old black burro, there is no one left for me to argue with about the geographical limits of the Southwest. Dobie included most of Texas and none of California; Robinson just the opposite; whereas Ainsworth said that wherever the mesquite grew, there was the Southwest—until I reported seeing mesquite in London's Kew Gardens.

As for my Southwest, I have always declared that the heart of it lies in New Mexico and Arizona and that the rest is merely marginal. I even went so far as to make a geodetic survey and locate the heart of hearts at the Santa Fe station in Albuquerque, there at the site of The Alvarado. When barbarians with bulldozers destroyed that most beautiful of the Fred Harvey houses, I relocated the *cor cordium* west southwest at El Morro, that great buff-colored battlement on which passing travelers from the time of Don Juan de Oñate have incised those poignant words *Pasó por aqui.*

This was the land of Nueva España through which Coronado marched in 1540 in search of the fabled Golden Cities of Cibola.

Alas for his lust, they proved to be only the mud pueblos of the Zuñis, engilded by the rising and setting sun.

Years passed before the Spaniards returned. Then it was for God not Gold that Padre Kino came to the Pimeria Alta, now known as Northern Sonora and Southern Arizona. There at the Papago *rancheria* of Bac on the Santa Cruz above Tucson, he founded a mission in the name of St. Francis Xavier. The church we call today the White Dove of the Desert, most beautiful of the Spanish mission churches, was built after Kino's time by the Franciscans.

During my year's work on the bicentennial book on Arizona, I steeped myself in the history of the Southwest, relived its epics, identified with its heroes, and ignored the shoot-out at the O.K. Corral and other frontier shenanigans. My friend Jim Serven is right when he writes that it was guns that pacified the West, yet no gun ever gave soul to a place. One burning day last summer, craving the coolness of coast, I launched out on the stream of history that flows west northwest from Tucson. It was the same stream that in the seventeenth century bore Kino to his discovery that California was *not* an island. *California no es ysla,* concluded the Jesuit pioneer in drawing his epochal map of the Golden Land. It was the same stream that in the next century carried Juan Bautista de Anza and his colonists to the Pacific and the founding of San Francisco.

Along this route that came to be known as the Gila Trail, Kearny rode in 1846 to consolidate the conquest of California and the Southwest. Close behind him lumbered Cooke and his 400 Mormon volunteers, blazing the first wagon road to the Pacific. They provisioned in Tucson, then hurried down the Santa Cruz to junction with the Gila.

There they found the Pimas at peace. So taken was Cooke with one nubile daughter of the tribe that on December 22 he confided to his journal: "I rode up to a group of women, men and girls. These last, naked above the hips, were of every age and pretty. It was a gladdening sight, of so much cheerfulness and happiness. One little girl particularly, by a fancied resemblance, excited much interest with me. She was so joyous that she seemed very innocent and pretty. I could not resist tying a red silk handherchief on her head for a turban; then, if perfect happiness ever dwells momentarily on earth, it seemed that it was with her."

No such distraction arrested me in Casa Grande, and I went on down the Gila to Yuma. There at the crossing of the Colorado I slept lightly for the shades of the past that never sleep. Here in olden times before the river was dammed, the crossing was not without peril. In spring the stream spread out to the width of half a mile. In winter it was fringed with ice. Here Anza and his colonists, Kearny and his dragoons, Cooke and his volunteers crossed the river. Garcés was martyred here. Martha Summerhayes came through Yuma in the 1870s, traveling by riverboat with her husband to his post at Fort Whipple near Prescott. It was in August and the temperature was 120 degrees. Behind the boat in an open barge the soldiers suffered and two of them died from the heat.

In the morning before the day's furnace was fully blasted, I reconnoitered the west bank off the river as far as the dams at Laguna and Imperial. I lay my fondness for southwestern dams to heredity. In the summer of 1909 my father who was then a horticulturist with the Bureau of Plant Industry of the U.S. Department of Agriculture, came to the Yuma crossing to inspect the new dam at Laguna. It was the first of the barriers across the Colorado, an Indian weir-type dam which led to the reclamation of the desert on both sides of the river.

It was dusty, he wrote of his drive upriver behind a four-mule wagon-team, and so hot at night that he slept outdoors on a cot at the Yuma Barracks. Today the mules are gone, the heat and the dust remain. And Laguna Dam is obsolete, the task of slowing the flow having been assumed by the later Imperial Dam, a very model of a modern waterworks. There the river is partly diverted through desilting basins and channeled by the All American Canal to the fertile fields of the Imperial Valley. The wild river is docile, its history unknown to the camperized crowds.

Beyond the river the road surmounts the honey-colored, wind-sculptured dunes and seeks the mountains, then climbs them in a marvel of engineering. In 1846 Cooke's wagon train had no road at all. So narrow and rocky was the defile they ascended, so impervious to pick and shovel, that the wagons had to be taken apart and carried through in pieces. That man Cooke ranks with Kino and Anza in my pantheon of Southwestern heroes. Today in Salt Lake City the only statue of a Gentile is the one of Philip St. George Cooke, leader of the Mormon Battalion.

In summertime the 4,000-foot summit of the Lagunas is bright with red sage and the deep orange of California poppies, beside which the Arizona variety is a pale yellow. There is also a stand of red shanks *(Adenostoma sparsifolium)*, that infrequent component of the chaparral which occurs also in the Santa Monica Mountains back of Malibu. So swift and smooth runs the ribbon of Interstate 8 that history is left behind and not rejoined until the highway descends to San Diego, a now great city under what is charitably called "coastal overcast."

There on the bay I met the shade of Dana, reliving the passionate experiences that so heated up *Two Years Before the Mast* that its prose goes on glowing into its second century. Not all of him went into it. He was a prudish Bostonian, his editor even more so. If it were not for a letter of reminiscence, written to Dana years later from one of his franker shipmates who had come upon the published sea story, we would not know that the virile young Yankee had "shacked up" on the beach with the same desirable nubility that had entranced Cooke upon the Gila.

Driving up coast I had no chance to reflect on history or anything else. Eyes front, belt tight, CHP observed. I had been away a year. There were changes, especially beyond Zuma Beach where I dropped out for a week. Warehouse-type residences built overpoweringly on narrow lots. And a rash of high risers that are making southwestern cities, from Albuquerque through Phoenix and Tucson to Los Angeles, so much the same. Santa Fe has had the good sense to stay close to earth.

Twenty years had passed since we staked out our claim on the cliff's edge. The old house was older, the trees taller, the neighbors closer. Coming from the desert's low humidity my bronchials found the damp air unfriendly. In the early morning chill I sat by a fire of oak to mesquite, hearing the low sky drip on tiles and leaves, as I let my Scripto lead me into another day.

At UCLA to which I was magnetized by books and friends, the changes were enormous. Fifty years ago as Occidental College students we had only scorn for the big new buildings on the bare hills of Westwood. Now masterful landscaping by the late Ralph Cornell has enveloped them in a green setting of great beauty.

Earlier in Tucson I had read Jack Smith's alert that the UCLA Gypsy Wagon was threatened by Progress. I checked it out. Still safe. There under the sycamores and jacarandas beside the limestone woman by Eric Gill (which I prefer to the rest of the Franklin Murphy Sculpture Garden's many riches), I savored a serenity coast and city have lost. Students were happier, girls prettier, coffee hotter. I could have stayed there forever at the calm heart of the whirlwind.

Without the classification scheme that organizes the millions of volumes in the University Research Library, I would have wandered helplessly in the vast stacks. Its call number led to a single book, one that had passed through my hands when, nearly forty years ago, I first came to UCLA and grasped the bottom rung of the ladder with only up to go. There it had waited patiently for a reader to whom it would be the book of books. I was that reader.

A hard-nosed administrator would deem wasteful the cost of housing books that may wait many years before they are wanted. Yet this is one of the functions of a research library—to have what is wanted when it is wanted. And so I carried my treasure to a remote corner of the stacks and there, dog with bone, I nibbled and made notes.

Later I called on Henry Miller, friend of half a century whom I had not seen since his eightieth birthday celebration at UCLA nearly four years ago. He was as alert and joyous as ever. How we talked!—clear back to 1931 when we first met on the staircase of the Faculty of Letters in the Burgundian capital of Dijon.

We made our way forward to the time when we lived in Beverly Glen and I ran a kind of bookmobile service from UCLA to feed Miller's huge appetite for books. He recalled an evening after arriving from France and Greece when we savored one of Fay's casseroles, artfully concocted on a post-Depression budget. Warmed by food and wine and friendship, he had embarked on one of his fabulous monologues on life, landscape and literature, and roamed the room with glass in hand, toasting the cook and the world at large.

Although then a neophyte librarian, I also regarded myself as a writer; and the hand that Henry Miller extended was the hand I clasped again last summer.

"So you are now at the University of Arizona," he mused as I rose to leave. "I was there once years ago, heading west for the first time. I stopped over in Tucson and found the university and stood there at the main gates. Big iron ones. Still there? Good. They were beautiful gates. Well, I stood a long time. Do you know what I almost did? You'll never believe it. Almost enrolled in the College of Agriculture." At that point Miller laughed and I said, "It was a cow college then. Mostly agriculture and mining."

"I was a kid," Miller resumed, "it was in 1913. I was only twenty. Never knew what lay ahead."

"Who does at that age? Now when I was a saxophone player on the S.S. *President Harrison.* . . . "

After packing a year's visiting into two weeks, all the way from Riverside to Capistrano, I was ready to resume the quiet life on the desert. Driving back I wondered what would have happened if Henry Miller had become an Arizona farmer. Would he also have become a writer and written a "Tropic of Tucson"?

I too came to the University of Arizona at twenty. The Occidental College Tigers played the Wildcats. We bit them and they clawed us, as we split a doubleheader. The first game was played in a dust storm with visibility near zero, and the Arizonans had the advantage of special goggles that enabled them to see in the murk. On the morrow, however, the visibility was the usual sixty miles and we batted the ball over the Rincons.

That was a dream team Oxy fielded in the 1920s, coached by Wilkie Clark. The battery of Bud Teachout and "Rats" Brobst was supported by Solly Mishkin at first, Rainier Mandel at second, Les Haserot at short, and Shigeo Tanaka at third, with an outfield of sluggers including the late Mike Godet.

Last year in Phoenix I encountered Lawson Smith, the retired president of Mountain Bell. It seemed that he saw that doubleheader of fifty years ago, having been the sports editor of the *Arizona Daily Wildcat*. I was able to hold my own in the exchange of recollections until he began quoting the batting averages of both teams.

"How come you remember them?" I asked him.

"I was always good at numbers," he explained. "That's why I got along well with the telephone company."

And what did I play on that stellar Oxy team? I was the batboy.

NORMAN CORWIN

H E TURNED RADIO on its ear in the 1930s and 1940s. There was no writer-director who matched the weekly original radio-play output of Norman Corwin. Poetry, illusion, humor, and provocative themes influenced a generation of those who tuned in—and there were many. At the end of World War II, he climaxed his presentations with *On a Note of Triumph,* an epic theater piece that dramatized the casualties of war and hailed the arrival of peace. Ensuing years gave way to television. Corwin turned his talents to the new medium and to film and theater.

Cut to the 1970s. Our staff was discussing the need of a media column. I suggested Norman Corwin, who was a family friend. My editor, Davis Dutton, approved. We arranged a meeting. Corwin was very cordial but only vaguely interested. Certainly he did not want to review TV. Neither did we. We explained that a monthly magazine is planned some three months in advance, precluding coverage of up-to-the-minute events. What we hoped for was a commentator, not a reviewer. One who could bring a frame of reference to the current media scene. We knew he was accustomed to speaking to a large audience. Our publication reached over a million readers. He perked up, but quickly erected a fence.

Norman Corwin

He would have to establish his own format to run the range of areas of communication without restraints. We knocked down the fence. He would be free. Style and content were up to him. Try it, we urged. If it didn't work, he could bow out. It worked. "Corwin on Media" became a monthly highlight. The reader response to his multifarious essays was a "rave."

A short time later, Dutton left the magazine to graze in greener pastures. I continued on as editor and attended to Corwin's perfectionist needs. He covered the spectrum of media. Somehow he tied his many interests to the media—language, newspapers, television, drama, poetry, puns, art, music, sports, politics. No subject eluded his reflective eye.

Corwin was an amiable contributor and was persuaded to do an occasional feature in addition to his monthly column. But he was a worrier about his work. He moaned and groaned in mock horror whenever we had to cut lines in the interest of space and sent detailed letters of instruction in the path of his submissions, especially when he was out of town. For example:

> July 17, 1973 (Idyllwild, Ca.)
> Dear Fran:
> I have the usual errata follow-up to my column, and I beg your kind indulgence.
> Page 2, bottom line: my carbon copy reads "Aroma mabrosial" when it should of course read "Aroma ambrosial." But then I ran off the carbon paper in the original typing and it may possibly be correct in the version I mailed you.
> Page 4, five lines from the end of paragraph 2: it now reads "to read this highly specialized" &c it should read "to seek *out* this highly specialized" &c.
> Page 4, last line of Pg. 2; please change "Spanish language" to "Spanish tongue."
> Page 5. Second line from the bottom of the page, please check to see that the printer or proofreader does not correct my "varicose" to read "various." Varicose is what I intend.
> I have been bitten by a red ant, and gave myself a 3rd degree

burn on an electric coil while attempting to cook for myself. An enormous blister on my left palm. As you can see, I am having a wonderful time here in the purple mountain majesties. From which perch I send you, as always, my love. Norman.

ps—My carbon reads on the last line of page 1, "an unim-peachabee name." You understand this refers to a bee which cannot be thrown out of office for illegal bugging, or breaking and entering a blossom. Just wanted to clear that up.

Another letter followed, same date—7.17.73

Would you please check on the name of Ditters Van Dittersdorf? I'm not sure whether it's a Van or a Von, and I don't have my reference library at hand. Also if you feel we need Nabokov's first name, please pop it in. I couldn't remember whether it is Vladimir or Jack.

Since I am faintly paranoid about the mails, would you send me assurances that this column arrived—and on time?

We almost never went to press without his last-minute instructions, and he almost never let us down:

3.18.74
Dear Fran:
Sorry to be early again. I know this can be demoralizing, and sets a bad precedent, but I will make up for it.

Four lines from the bottom of p. 5 you will find the phrase, "happy, whappy environment." There being no such word as whappy in the language, some Young Turk on your staff, or the typesetter, or proofreader, may decide to edit it.

Please advise any of same, that if the word is changed, I will personally come down and whap them. But not you. . . . "

And again:

Dear Francesca:
Why am I so good to you? I made this column a little longer than usual, to help fill the spaces left by the absence of auto ads.

I write this on the 75th anniversary of my Royal typewirter. It stopped spelling correctly when it reached 70. I have even seen it trasnpose letters in wrods. How awful, the aging process. Still, when you consider the alternative. . . .

In July of 1980, he went to Hawaii to lecture. We received our usual communiqué:

> Dear Francesca:
> Yesterday I flew to the island of Kauai and had a wonderful day gorging on the extraordinary beauties of the place. The terrain, I mean, not the dames. I took some pictures, but my camera began acting strangely in the film-forwarding mechanism, and I just hope it is not all one miserable jumble. Unfortunately my teaching schedule here does not give me time to do the groundwork for the kind of feature article we discussed before I left, so I may just turn in some nice pictures of the Clouds of Hawaii, of which I am an infatuate. (I know you are tempted to call me infatuate-headed, but please restrain yourself.)
>
> If Writer's Block [his column] hasn't gone to press yet, the attached version which dispensed with abbreviations, is the one I prefer. Absolutely the last change. . . .

We communicated by phone most of the time, but followup letters became part of the routine. I looked forward to his final gem-polishing, and the nit-picking was made tolerable by the good humor he had about himself and his work. Many of the columns are collected in a book he called *Holes in a Stained Glass Window,* which title quotes a cab driver who said, "The trouble with stained glass windows is you can't see through them. You have to punch holes in it."

Little did that cab driver realize how apt an analogy the stained glass window was to Corwin, who fastidiously pieces words together of ranging colors and meaning to fit the larger design of his work. No holes necessary.

■

Corwin on Media
In the Racks

If there is no browsing in heaven, I don't want to go there. I hardly expect to reach the Reservation on my own merits, but if through some clerical error at the gate I find myself in paradise with eternity on my hands and nothing to do, I would ask for the nearest library, bookdealer, record shop or art gallery; and if there are no such establishments along the empyreal malls, I would ask to be transferred.

None of us can tell what diversions there may be in Celestial City, but the pleasures of browsing in this life are well known. The dominion of books is so vast, and browsing in it so commonplace, they do not even bear remark. But perhaps less familiar to the general browser are the happy hunting grounds of the record shops. If you are patient enough, and don't give up because there may be no quick yield, sooner or later you are bound to come across treasures in the bins and racks—mostly older items which have gone unnoticed by reviewers and buyers, or which may have been forgotten. Allow me to share a few of these with you—items I gathered across the years, by chance encounter.

Take the case of a *Music in Africa* series on a London label, recorded by an Englishman named Hugh Tracey as a set of eight 10-inch discs. The first cut on side one of *Kenya,* is "Chemirocha," sung by nubile girls of the Kipsigi tribe after hearing a gramophone record by the American cowboy singer Jimmy Rogers. To their ear, Jimmy Rogers was Chemirocha; they were so taken by his style that they decided to celebrate him with a song inviting him to dance with them. According to Tracey, the men of the district were not quite as excited about Chemirocha as their women, but the girls said, "Aha, this is no ordinary creature—this is a faun, half man and half antelope!" And they sang to him through a soloist, assisted by a shy and intermittent chorus, to the twanging of a chepkong lyre. The song is so pure, so charming, so utterly ingenuous as to be touching, and it makes you wonder whether, in the decades since these maidens raised their sweet hymn to Chemirocha, there remains anything at all of such openhearted, undissimulating simplicity in the far reaches of that troubled continent.

Across the world from Kenya, in a little shop on a crowded street in Shanghai just before the great takeover, I once picked up a dozen 10-inch, 78-rpm recordings of music then popular in urban China. I could not make out the labels because they were printed in Chinese, but they were a mixed bag . . . some were highly westernized, some as Oriental as ginseng, one sounded like a Scotch folk song, another seemed like a version of the "Volga Boat Song" but wasn't; there was a slam-bang samba, and a children's song. But one which commended itself to me especially for its liveliness and lilt was a song whose opening words, in Chinese of course, sounded very much like "Make way, make way." I brought these discoids back with me to New York, and proposed to some friends in the music world that the "Make way" number might, with fresh and understandable lyrics, make a good popular song for this country. I was patted on the head and told to go run along and write scripts and leave music to musicians. But apparently I was not the only American who visited China that summer, because somebody brought back that same record and was *not* patted on the head; and about two years after I had tried to push the song, it not only turned up in the U.S., but vaulted to Number One on the Hit Parade, under the title of "Rose, Rose, I Love You." It led the parade for many weeks.

Considerably east of Shanghai, in a record shop in Sherman Oaks, I came across a violin concerto by Giovanni Viotti (d. 1824) on a Westminster label. I had never heard of the composer, which is in itself not significant, because several shelves of expensive encyclopedias could be filled with things I don't know. But this concerto, No. 22 in A minor, was also unknown to recording orchestras until this release. The liner on the album commented in passing, "One cannot refrain from saying it is strange no other recording of this work has preceded this one." Strange indeed, when you consider that the prodigious violinist Joseph Joachim used to play it privately, with his friend Brahms at the piano, for their mutual pleasure; and that Brahms quoted Joachim as saying the concerto "made him happy that such beautiful music is to be found in the world." With all that going for it, the wonder is that it took so long to get it down on records, and that to this day it is seldom (if ever) heard in concert. Happily, two recordings of the Viotti have been made since the Westminster—one by Philips, the other by Turnabout.

Re this same Joachim, the rod scope of my ignorance included unawareness of the fact that he was himself a composer. Recently in the Sam Johnson Bookshop on Westwood Boulevard, after loading up on some books I was seeking, I came across a carton of used LP recordings on top of a table. Often there is something faintly leprous about used record albums in shops—the jackets are scuffed, the finish no longer glossy, the disc itself looks weary, there are marks of age about the eye, or hole of the disc, and maybe a scratch or two on the surface. I fanned through the stack idly, since I was not bargain-hunting, and already owned most of the major works of major composers, as well as a lot of minor ones; but lo, here was an album, in good shape, too, of *Hungarian Concerto*, Op. 11, by Joachim. I took it home and played it. It has a second movement, a *romanze*, of very great beauty. And, like the text on the Viotti jacket, this liner had a complaint concerning "the almost total neglect" of Joachim's writing. The album is *Candide;* the soloist, Aaron Rosand; the orchestra, that of Radio Luxembourg. It is the only recording of the work listed in Schwann. Then there are anthological oddities such as *The "A" Composers,* a piano recital by Barbara Lewis Golub, of short pieces by composers whose names begin with A: Arne, Antipoff, Arensky, D'Albert, Albéniz, Allende, Aguilar, Auric, Alexandrovitch and D'Agreves. It seems an odd basis for an anthology—but why not? Especially since several of the works have unique features: for example, Thomas Arne's *Sonata in F Major* is in three move-ments—andante, adagio and allegro—but the adagio consists only of a two-bar interlude that takes 14 seconds to play, and leads directly to an allegro in waltz tempo. Then there is a wonderfully slinky *Orientale* by the Russian Nicholas Amani (d. 1904), which is reminiscent of the Slavo-Arabic meld in certain pages of Tchaikovsky and Rimsky-Korsakov. The auspices of the recording are mysterious: no publisher is credited either on the jacket or label, beyond the code letters MC-201, 561.

Another curiosity, bearing the long title *Composers at the Keyboard Play Their Own Compositions,* is actually a second-generation recording: originally these performances by Grieg, Dohnányi, Saint-Saëns, Mascagni, D'Indy, Fauré, De Koven and Moritz Rosenthal, of selections from their own works, were made by them for the Ampico recording-piano, an instrument that is now museum stuff, but was once, in the early years of this century, much prized in living rooms rich enough to own them. The performances were stenciled on paper rolls, and were remarkable for their fidelity to the touch, dynamics and tempo of the pianist. *Composers at the Keyboard* is a kind of mini-gallery of musical history, the equivalent of daguerreotypes of masters of the near past (all died between 1907 and 1960). Grieg aficionados may be dismayed by his seemingly haphazard reading of two of his works ("his playing is unaffected and bubbles with almost childlike happiness," explains the liner, while at the same time acknowledging that Grieg "seems to bypass the note values in his own printed score"). But Saint-Saëns, who made his recording at the age of 70, is sprightly and eloquent in *Valse Langourese* and the finale from Act One of *Samson et Delila.* The Horowitz of the collection is Rosenthal, who challenges the virtuosity of the Ampico with brilliant execution of his *Carnaval da Vienne* and *Papillons.*

The mechanical piano (then called pianola) surfaces again in an album with an even longer title: *George Gershwin Conducts Excerpts from Porgy and Bess*—a Mark 56 label, produced by George Garabedian of Anaheim, specialist in vintage recordings. The record stars Gershwin, on side one, playing his own very early "Rialto Ripples" at breakneck speed, and an item called "Tee-Oodle-Um-Bum-Bo." On the same side is Gershwin's guest appearance on a Rudy Vallee radio program in 1932, in which the maestro plays brilliantly, and reads poorly a script prepared for him, with such exchanges as:

VALLEE: How much money do you make now, George?

GERSHWIN: About half as much as you do, Rudy. How much is that?

VALLEE: One third as much as I told you this afternoon.

Vallee then asks which of his "show tunes" he prefers; Gershwin replies, "This one," and plays "I've Got Rhythm" with his usual electricity. But the feature of the recording is a rehearsal of *Porgy and Bess* on July 19, 1935, in which we hear Gershwin, as conductor, directing orchestra and singers.

Before I run out of space, let it be said that not all collector's items need be oddities—all it takes to make a curiosity is a gap in the collector's knowledge. Like my delight in discovering that Verdi had written a string quartet, and that it had been transcribed for string orchestra and recorded handsomely by Steinberg and the Pittsburgh. And then there are all those tinkerings, parodies and modern arrangements of Bach. To name just a few from my own hoard, there is *Jazz Guitar Bach* by André Benichou and his Well-Tempered Three (Nonesuch); a quite silly comedy album called *Baroque Americana* (Mace), which includes "Yea-Zoo Joy on the Range" and "Sheep May See Nelly Home Safely"—amalgams of Bach and old American tunes. But for me the very finest liberties taken with Bach are those of William Mallochin *The Art of Fuguing* (TownHall). As for the joys of collecting genuine Bach—the whole family—don't get me started.

At Home With Captain Bligh
And the Bride of Frankenstein

BY NORMAN CORWIN

Sic transit Gloria Swanson. This ungallant jest (Gloria is only seventy-seven as this goes to press) occurred to me recently when, upon mentioning the name of Charles Laughton to a college writing class, a nineteen-year-old student asked, "Who was he?"

It took me a while to recover from the shock. I chose to think that the student had either alighted that morning from a flying saucer which had spent the last nineteen years in outer space, or he had never seen a vintage movie on TV. But then I asked myself whether it wâs simply a case of the frailty of celebrity, as suggested by the sublime Emily Dickinson when she wrote

> Fame is a bee.
> It has a song—
> It has a sting—
> Ah, too, it has a wing.

No: I was sure Laughton's fame is still alive in the hive, so it couldn't be that. And then I got to thinking about old Bligh as I drove home from that class; about the fascination Laughton still holds for millions of people (to be safe, I should say millions of people twenty and older), and about the privilege I enjoyed of knowing him and his wife, Elsa Lanchester, in the prime years.

I met the Laughtons in the course of directing a network radio series called "The Pursuit of Happiness"—a weekly all-star variety program on CBS. In those days, it was still possible for actors of the stature of the Laughtons to speak words written by writers of the stature of Thomas Wolfe and Stephen Vincent Benét on a commercial network. That is just what they did for me, through adaptations I made from *John Brown's Body*, and a melange of Wolfeiana. The experience was new for them, and they apparently enjoyed it to the extent that, in a burst of cordiality, they invited me to be their guest if I should ever go to Hollywood. When soon afterward I signed up to write a movie, I notified the Laughtons that I was coming to their part of the world, and back came a telegram: DOG HOUSE IN GARDEN ALL READY FOR YOU WHAT TIME DO YOU ARRIVE BECAUSE WE WANT TO MEET YOU.

It was my first trip to California, and I flew on the crack DC-3 *American Mercury*, pride of American Airlines, which took only eighteen hours to make it from New York to Burbank. I was met at Lockheed terminal by Charles and Elsa, and they drove straight to their home on North Rockingham in Brentwood. It was the kind of house a star should live in: gracious, spacious, thick-walled in the Spanish manner, and bepooled. It had an upstairs, downstairs, lady's chamber, master's chamber, a garden, a secretary named Renee Ruben whom they had imported from England, an Irish setter named Joe, a redwood dog house, and a guest house that was turned over to me. Palm and banana-tree fronds framed most of the windows; there was green everywhere, and a profusion of scentless roses.

As soon as I installed my bags, Charles and Elsa insisted on showing me the city and the countryside and the sea. We drove on or past streets bearing musical Spanish names—La Cienega, La Brea (it was better not to know they meant marsh and tar). Cahuenga, Figueroa, Alvarado. For a paleface brought up on names like Boston and Greenfield and Springfield, California was already exotic.

Next came lunch at an establishment unlike anything on the eastern seaboard, the departmented cornucopia of Farmer's Market, thronged and prosperous. Then out to the Pacific shore, and inland across the Malibu highlands through parched canyons, down to San Fernando Valley. Here stood walnut and orange groves where now eight-lane freeways are ribbons of smog in the sunlight; here were farms where now vast shopping complexes, each the size of ancient Athens, spread themselves opulently at Topanga, Panorama, and Fashion Square.

The Laughtons were easy to live with. We would have breakfasts together, attended as well by Renee the secretary; then Charles would go to the Paramount studio, and I to RKO or CBS, since I was working for both, and we would again gather at dinner, al- most always served at home. It is to the glory of Laughton's mem- ory that he was not a Hollywood mixer, a partygoer, a bookkeeper of social accounts and balances. He and Elsa preferred the company of books and paintings, and their few loyal friends were invariably independent and un-Hollywood people like themselves: Jean Renoir and his wife Dido, Frank Lloyd Wright, Jack and Louise Moss, Iris Barry, Joseph Losey (not yet the eminent film director he was to become), Ruth Gordon and, later, Bertholt Brecht.

Miss Ruben, much more English in mien and accent than her employers, was as outspoken as they on subjects esthetic, domestic and political; conversations around the bar after dinner were always loud, roaming, irreverent, supercharged with prejudices, occasionally informed, often funny, and sequined with elegant profanity. Typical was an evening spent in a free-for-all on the subject of symbolism in movies. Charles and Elsa held, against Renee and myself, that screenwriters had no business using indirection in the telling of a story. "Actors were meant to act," Charles complained, "and not to have inanimate objects tell stories for them." I argued that he was being no more than a lobbyist for the special interest of the actor; that symbolism was basic to all art; that every word written or spoken is a symbol, and that literalism was a prosaic god for him to be worshipping.

Except in the company of friends, Laughton was inclined to be shy and uncertain of any subject except theater, painting and sculpture, on which he had instant and eloquent opinions. He backed up his opinions with a house full of paintings, so many that I wrote a commentary and presented it to him:

> This is a house of art
> In every part:
> In the master's can,
> Cezanne;
> On the kitchen wall,
> Maillol;
> Wherever you park your ass, O,
> It's under a Picasso . . .

and so on for Utrillo and Miró and Dufy and Soutine. The prize of his collection was Renoir's *Judgment of Paris,* which he had bought for $35,000. There was occasion, once, to clean the Renoir. It looked fine to me as it hung, but then I was no connoisseur of soiled impressionists. The very thought of a masterpiece being sent to a cleaner's chilled me, until Charles explained that the materials for deterging a painting—especially a valuable one—were soap and water, and that the work would be done right at home.

In this period, Charles was in the process of collecting pre-Columbian sculpture, and he had both good taste and good contacts in the enterprise. He also loved primitives, and was as proud of his Horace Pippins and Papsdorfs as of his color study for *La Grande Jatte* by Seurat, and his Morris Graves. Papsdorf was a milkman, and Charles told how, when he went to see him in Detroit and bought some paintings, Papsdorf said on parting, "Well, thanks for the business."

The Laughtons seldom entertained. In the three months of my stay, I remember only the novelist Louis Bromfield coming to dinner, and that was in connection with a film based on one of Bromfield's books. Much of the talk that night had to do with California as a place in which to live, work and paint. Bromfield held that there was no such thing as a truly blue sky in Southern California—that it was at best a bleached blue gray, even when the sun was shining hard. Charles was curiously irked. He loved California, and took it personally that Bromfield disparaged its skies.

The house in Brentwood was by no means hermetically sealed against visitors. Every now and then Charles's and Elsa's film and stage associates (Elsa was appearing as chief *diseuse* at the Turnabout Theater in Hollywood) would drift in and out; but there was never a party of any kind, never more than six or seven people under the roof at any one time. Though their next-door neighbor was Thomas Mann, there was never any exchange; nor, so far as I knew, did they ever meet. Only on one occasion was any notice taken of the Manns, and that was on July 4th, when someone on the Mann side of the dividing hedge kept shooting fireworks all day, to the annoyance of the Laughtons and the fury of Miss Ruben.

Personal or emotional matters were never discussed in the household, at least not within my hearing, and there was never any table talk or after-dinner scuttlebutt about themselves or the private lives of their friends. Several times they met a girl I was involved with, but they had no more curiosity about her than they did about the gardener of the Manns next door, or the Manns themselves. On art and politics—their own and that of friends—they could be vocal and sharp: the rest was lost in a kind of circumspection that I took to be part of the British character.

Once I tried to get Charles interested in music. He had had hardly any exposure to it, and I maintained that music, as sister to drama, poetry, painting and sculpture, had every claim to his attention; that he was missing not only a treasury of pleasure, but an important element in the promptuary of the actor. I bought recordings of Mozart, Haydn, Beethoven, Brahms, Bach, Schubert, De Falla, Lalo, Sibelius, Tchaikovsky, Shostakovich. He listened patiently, found Mozart too effeminate, Lalo's *Symphonie Espagnole* too confectionary, allowed some talent in Beethoven's *Rasoumovsky Quartets,* professed to understand Sibelius and Shostakovich. But either I was a poor instructor or Charles a poor pupil; he remained indifferent to music and at times hostile.

Poetry was another matter. Charles needed no guidance *there.* He had an ear acutely tuned to cadence and nuance, and a probing and imperious intelligence when it came to language. In radio, only Orson Welles and Martin Gabel were in the same class when it came to handling rhetoric and language that flexed the imagination. Midway in another CBS series, I produced, on three successive weeks, *An American Trilogy,* consisting of adaptations of Wolfe, Sandburg and Whitman. I had no hesitation whatever about casting Laughton, an Englishman, to be cicerone to material as American as hotdogs and the Tea Party, for he had the capacity to be as colloquial or lyrical as the texts required, along with other qualities between, above and beyond.

But one day, when we were preparing the Whitman broadcast, I found him copying by hand the entire typescript of the program, including Whitman's verse.

"Why are you doing that?" I asked.

He went into a long, quasi-occult explanation of a theory that, by writing out sentences as special as Whitman's, the very transmittal of words from his eyes to his arm to his hand to his fingers and then to paper, would so deeply instill the language in him that it would become embedded in his subconscious, hence he would be able absolutely to master it. I knew very well that he would master it without any elaborate process, but by this time he had already labored so hard, and was so earnest about his theory, that I shrugged and waited until he had finished transcribing thirty-six pages; then we got to work.

Charles had a special insight into the Sandburg script, because he had earlier met the poet during a rehearsal of one of my broadcasts (not a Laughton show) in New York. I had known Sandburg for some years, and he happened to be in town from Michigan for a week, and dropped by to say hello. Coincidentally so did Laughton, who with Elsa had just that afternoon arrived by ship from a holiday in Europe. The meeting of these two for the first time under such circumstances was so singular that I broke rehearsal in order that we could savor the occasion. Sandburg had seen most of Laughton's films, and Laughton had read most of Sandburg's poetry, and they professed mutual admiration. "But one film I missed," said Sandburg, "was your *Ruggles of Red Gap.* As a biographer of Lincoln, I wish I had seen you do the Gettysburg Address. Didn't you speak it in the movie?"

"Indeed I did," answered Laughton, "and I'm going to do it again for you right now." And then and there, with just the three of us in a Madison Avenue studio, Laughton performed the Address.

When the holidays rolled around at the end of that year, Charles presented me with the then new six-volume Sandburg biography of Lincoln. Inside the cover of the first volume he had written, "In cherished memory of a cherished experience with the author of this work."

To myself as friend and co-worker, there was little in Charles's offscreen demeanor that resembled the Laughton known to movie audiences. The unchallengeable authority of his Captain Bligh, Henry VIII, Rembrandt, Javert, Papa Barrett, Nero and other powerful screen performances was not part of his breakfast table, living room or radio-studio character. On first meeting him, I expected a tough, demanding actor, aware of his global fame and formidable stature in show-biz. Instead he was mild, eager to listen and be directed, open to suggestion, and only occasionally intractable—when he was afraid he was beyond his depth or wanted to cover a weakness with bluster. As he had very few craft weaknesses, he did not often need to exercise this reflex. If onstage he were unsure of himself, he indulged in bad habits—a clumsy coyness, excessive blinking, a petulant air. But in a radio studio there was no point to eye-blinks.

Elsa, on the other hand, was as close to her onstage image as Charles was distant from his. The same piquancy, frizzled red hair, dimpled chin, thinker's brow, and large brown eyes that seemed to mock even when she idled in neutral. She could be caustic, and had a Hogarthian sense of caricature that was especially active in her songs of soubrettes and simple sinners. She had no compunction about ridiculing what she considered my more conspicuous foibles, and nothing was too small to escape comment. She noticed, for example, that if I cut a finger, I would apply a Band-Aid to keep the wound clean. This struck her as finicky and ludicrous, and she coined the opprobrious term "tidgy-bandage" to describe overcaution. Once she complained of difficulty in swallowing, and I, having years back had the same thing and gone to a doctor who diagnosed it as a harmless condition called globus hystericus, told her what I thought it was. She shrieked with laughter, then indignantly accused me of implying that she was hysterical. I tried to assure her that the term had nothing to do with common hysteria, but she would not be mollified. At length she went to a doctor, was told she had globus hystericus, and promptly recovered from it.

While Charles is remembered for the wide range of his characterizations, Elsa's own versatility tends to be overlooked. She caroms with the greatest of ease from the bride of Frankenstein (she also played a very straight Mary Shelley, *author* of the classic, in an introduction to the film) to queens (Anne of Cleves in *Henry VIII*), barmaids, aunts, dotty dowagers; she is at home in Westerns, easterns, sci-fi, whodunits (*The Spiral Staircase, Witness for the Prosecution*); and she has also directed for the stage (Theater West). She is in firm command of a many-splendored talent, and speaks, when she has a mind to, in torrents of articulateness.

Over the years there have been several biographies of Laughton published, one of them recently. They are, alas, mostly workaday. The first was written during Laughton's lifetime by a scribe who, according to Elsa, never took the trouble to meet his subject or check his manuscript for accuracy. Charles was so scornful of the work that when people sent him copies of it for his autograph he would return the books unsigned.

The definitive biography will probably have to come from Elsa.

She writes well, and knows the ground. If and when such a book comes out, I will buy a copy and send it to the college student who asked me who Charles Laughton was.

If I can remember who the student was.

ANAÏS NIN

FOR MANY LITERARY women of my generation, Anaïs Nin was the model to emulate. Her focus on interior feelings and her breakthrough in writing about them embraced our frustrations. She inspired us to examine our roles in the arts and to experiment with our creative ideas. I watched her from afar and read anything of hers that was available. It was years before publishers were willing to risk their money on her unconventional subject matter. How fortunate that she lived to see a complete reversal of their earlier defective vision.

Many invitations came to my editor's desk. One was to a screening of a documentary called *Anaïs Observed*, produced by Robert Snyder. I went with preconceived impressions. The documentary reinforced those impressions. This was a portrait of grace and strength and beliefs. After the film, it was announced that Nin was present. Immediately, a line formed to greet her. I joined the line.

Slim and delicate in a long, silvery dress, she greeted friends and fans with equal pleasure, or so it seemed. When it came my turn, I introduced myself, told her how much I liked the film and admired her writing. I did not want to hog the line, as many others were waiting, but could I phone her to talk one day? She looked at me for a moment with friendly but penetrating eyes as if to evaluate my legitimacy, then asked for a piece of paper and pen, wrote down her phone number, and said, "Call me."

Her house was a small, artfully designed modern structure, with a view of the Silver Lake Reservoir. The architect was Lloyd Wright, a relative by marriage. Here, she could retreat and work in serenity high above Los Angeles and in the company of her attentive husband, Rupert Pole. We had instant rapport and talked of many things: writers and writing, music (her brother was a musician and so was mine), siblings, women and children. We shared attitudes about women who tried to gain recognition for their particular talents, who pursued careers not open to them, and who needed to feel the support of other women. She was not a feminist in a political sense, but she represented the ideal of feminism. Confidence in her dreams, she said, made them come true.

Why did she choose to settle in Los Angeles, after New York and Paris—cities that abounded in sophistication and artistic energy? Would that be a good subject for an article? She agreed. So we started our friendship.

We exchanged no letters, but met from time to time at her home for tea or lunch, or talked on the phone. And then the cancer that she had fought for some ten years ran rampant. I visited her at the hospital. When she died, I wrote a short tribute. In lieu of correspondence, I set it down here, for it best expresses my feelings about her.

■

In the course of a lifetime, there are a few people who touch you with their spirit and leave you forever clothed in the grace of their visit. Anaïs Nin was such a person. Delicate and strong, spiritual and worldly, neurotic and serene—a collage of opposites. She challenged convention, developed an introspective style of fiction writing and made literary history in her time.

She died in January of this year and the shock of sadness to those who knew her was seismic. She would have been seventy-four on

Anaïs Nin

February 21. Only in the last ten years of her life did she gain recognition. And today, the writing that was rejected by major publishers in the Thirties and Forties and accepted only by an avant-garde coterie is still new and vital and leaves a ribbon of readers and imitators around the world.

She was a supreme diarist. Her journey through the "inner spaces," fused with daily reflections, transcended the limits of autobiography. The diary provided a form in which she could write as a woman without compromising. So clear was her understanding of self (years of psychoanalysis helped) that she could retain her exquisite femininity without having to underplay her intellect; that she could give hope and emotional nourishment to men and women.

Some three years ago, I asked Anaïs Nin if she would write an article for us to launch our Westways Women series. Though she was not of the West she did choose to come here after Paris and New York, and in 1949 moved to Los Angeles.

She wrote, "A new style of life unknown to the East developed here. It was a style of harmony with nature." She found she could satisfy her "need for seclusion, for space, for intimacy with sea or mountain, with naturalness of dress and informality."

Later, she did two more articles—one on Bali that won the Pacific Travel Writers' Award and another on Noumea. It pleased her to do the travel pieces and play the role of a "working reporter." She reached out to new people and turned her fantasies of exotic places into reality.

The last year of her life she was ill almost continuously, but was not without faith. She worked a little each day, walked when she could, swam when she could. Even in the hospital, the room became *her* room with books and plants and bright wall hangings. Musicians came to play for her, poets came to read to her, friends to talk. She inspired that kind of devotion.

A week or so before Christmas, I phoned. She was at home and answered with her quaintly accented "hallo." The voice was very faint. "I don't seem to be getting any strength back," she said in a tone of disbelief.

"You will," I tried to reassure her.

46

But she never did.

Her devoted husband, Rupert Pole, said that they had talked about death, talked about her fear of going, of leaving him. When the time came she was ready to drift off. She wanted no funeral. He scattered her ashes over the Pacific as she desired. The winds and water have her now.

In one of her diaries she recorded, "The secret of a full life is to live and relate to others as if they might not be there tomorrow."

Today is that tomorrow. She is no longer here. Those who knew her cherish what she gave to every moment of friendship. If this seems to be rhapsodic, let it be. For Anaïs Nin evoked many kinds of music, the purity of a Handel sonata, the lilting harmony of Mendelssohn, the witty discord of Stravinsky. She left us her music and her magic.

March, 1977

■

Magic in Los Angeles

BY ANAÏS NIN

I first came to the West in 1949, seeking health and the sun. But I stayed because I found an atmosphere propitious for work. The social life is more relaxed. There are less pressures. Friends live far away from each other and if you need isolation and serenity and uninterrupted work you can have it.

Los Angeles has a way of hiding the more intimate, the more charming and personal aspects of the unique style of life it has developed. Having an open mind to innovations, experiments, new styles of thought and life, Los Angeles became sensitive to the caricatures made of it by hasty visitors. It concealed its creative, numinous life as native villages did in the jungle: behind trees, bushes, among rocks, lying deep in canyons; and superficial visitors never discovered its genuine beauty.

A new style of life, unknown to the East, developed here. It was a style of harmony with nature. The outside and inside of the house intermingled, grew in unison. Every window framed a tree, the sea, a pool or an inner flowering patio like the secret patios of the ancient Oriental cities.

There was a need for seclusion, for space, for intimacy with sea or mountains, with naturalness of dress and informality. It was the beginning of the ritual of grilling meat in the patio by the man of the house. Formal dress vanished and gave way to fantasy and playfulness.

What attracted so many to the West were the qualities that one attributes to a small village—fraternity between neighbors in their needs, the still human and personal relationships to postmen or shopkeepers. The large Mexican and Japanese populations imprinted some of their special qualities: The Mexicans created a more relaxed sense of time, a smiling graciousness; the Japanese influenced the style of gardening and the simplicity of the one-floor house opening on gardens.

It must have been this new, as yet uncreated world that attracted so many artists to the West. In the Thirties, Schoenberg and Stravinsky settled here, pleased with the reception the tolerant, open-minded West gave to the new sounds these composers were creating. Musicians like Heifetz and Piatigorsky found Los Angeles the gentle place to relax in between strenuous concert tours.

Many famous writers like Faulkner, Fitzgerald, Carson McCullers and James Agee came to write for the motion-picture studios. In the studio vaults lie many treasures, scripts not considered commercial in the Thirties or Forties, which would be admired today because of the changes in taste and consciousness that have taken place. Other writers remained to do serious work: Aldous Huxley, Thomas Mann, Christopher Isherwood and Henry Miller.

Lloyd Wright came in 1917 and designed the Hollywood Bowl and later the poetic Wayfarer's Chapel for the Disciples of Swedenborg. This was the only architectural wonder I heard discussed by fastidious Europeans.

In France we had an eccentric postman who asserted that the

only way to combat boredom during his monotonous rounds was to dream of and build a miniature castle. Here in Los Angeles we had an old Italian mason who, utilizing broken tiles, bottles and pottery, erected the Watts Towers, which reflect childhood memories of mosaics, plazas, campaniles, church belfries. When the city threatened to tear down the towers as unsafe, the sculptures were hotly defended by artists who know that the most unsafe thing of all is tearing down people's dreams.

Cornelia Runyon, the sculptress, carved her semiprecious stones on the terrace of her house above Zuma Beach, almost within reach of the spray, while a king snake slept peacefully under the eaves. I visited a potter's kiln on the deck of a houseboat. There is still a carousel on the Santa Monica pier which can be rented for parties. Above the carousel, artists live in studios shaped like towers, which give them a circular view of sea and mountains.

In Santa Monica Canyon, while Sam Francis paints the world's largest paintings in a cathedral-sized studio, his Japanese wife Mako makes pop art films.

Independent films, while financed by the studios, remain within the artistic control of the film maker. The dazzling *A Safe Place,* Hollywood's first surrealist film, written and directed by Henry Jaglom, is, in the words of Chris Mohr in England, "without owing anything to literature . . . the most perfectly attempted film equivalent of the novel's stream of consciousness."

Other artists make films on their own. Dancer Allegra Snyder made *Gestures of Sand,* capturing the unique quality of Margalit Oved's work. It is a "filmic exploration of some of the patterns of music, movement, ritual and myth which were integrally a part of the Jews of Aden," Margalit Oved's birthplace. The film conveys the intensity, beauty and strangeness of this unusual dancer.

Venice is the refuge of poor artists. When Harry Partch needed a place to house his many exotic, self-designed and self-built musical instruments, he found a vacant laundromat. The platform enabled him to expose his instruments to those who walked around it. Today, through a documentary film, *The Dream that Remains,* we can celebrate permanently the presence of this unique Californian. The film, directed by Stephen Pouliot and produced by Betty

Freeman, is a delight for all the senses. It evokes the color and forms of the instruments, their creation, the original music Harry Partch draws from them, interwoven with his adventurous life, his mischievous wit, his spontaneity.

It is here that Robert Snyder completed the full-length cinematic portrait, *Odyssey of Henry Miller*. This new biography gives so much more than the written ones—the voice, the gestures, the daily actions. Henry Miller is as relaxed and confiding before Snyder's camera as during the private visit of a friend.

When I first arrived I was, as any visitor, looking for confirmation of the Hollywood described by Nathanael West. This was a world of illusion created by the studios. Entire illusory cities—Western, Oriental, Parisian, Londonian.

I was not surprised to run into a wooden house being moved on wheels. It occupied the whole street and moved towards me with such ghostly unreality that I expected a party would be going on during the voyage, expected that the occupants, though surprised, had not allowed the evacuation to interrupt their lives. I visited the thrift shops which dress the impoverished extras waiting for film roles. I saw the people who make the papier-mâché statues for film décors, artificial plants, the costumes. I saw a New York subway station being moved, floating above the stream of cars. I saw a complete pissoir on a truck, with all its French theater posters, fresh and new, built too soon for the filming of *Tropic of Cancer*.

I heard stories: how the studios paid dearly for a reproduction of the Wayfarer's Chapel, more than it had cost to build; that veterans in a hospital, when asked whether they preferred the visit of an actor who, though famous for his war roles, had never been to the front, or an authentic war hero, chose the actor. But this was the movie-set Hollywood.

It is in the genuine Los Angeles that one discovers painter Judy Chicago, who carried out an experiment which has become history. She selected fifteen young women artists from California Institute of the Arts, and placed them in a mansion of fifteen rooms, which was given to them free for several months until it was time to tear it down. They called it Womanhouse and each young woman was given a room to furnish and decorate according to her fantasy. The only condition was that they had to do everything themselves, from scraping off the old paint to the carpentry and electrical work—every aspect of the creation of rooms representing their dreams. The results were astonishing. Each room was an original symbolic creation, a happening, an expression of woman's dream. Those who saw the rooms regretted the impermanency of them. Fortunately it was filmed by Joanna Demetrakas.

Women went on to create a permanent base for their activities, Womanspace, a house in Venice which became a center for art exhibits, conferences, rap sessions, showings of films by women and the publication of a journal dealing with the psychological, historical, and political problems of women.

Womanhouse started a precedent. From Womanhouse to Womanspace. Womanspace was not large enough. Last fall, the women took over the old Chouinard Art School and converted it into a women's building. It was named after the Women's Building at the 1883 World's Columbian Exposition in Chicago, which was designed by a woman architect, run by a board of lady managers, and filled with the work of women from all around the world. The new Women's Building will house Womanspace, Feminist Women Workshop, several women's art galleries, a feminist bookshop, and the Associated Women's Press. This includes Women in Films, started by Georganne Heller and Tichi Wilkerson to gain equal opportunity for women in the motion picture industry. Robert Hagel, president of the Burbank Studios, donated the premises of the Burbank Studios for their WIF meeting and for the fund-raising party of Cinewomen. He is a big promoter of the women's groups, and Mary Anne Trumerg, former schoolteacher, has checked into the Burbank Studios as the first female grip to be hired by a production company.

The atmosphere which made Paris such a center of creative life for centuries was the sense of freedom which encouraged experiments, innovation and individualism. It exists here. It has to be more self-generated because it has not yet crystallized, but one can observe the million active cells here and there, propelled by physical energy born of contact with nature, now seeking nourishment of another kind.

It is here that Carlos Castaneda writes his books exploring new states of consciousness, that Dory Previn writes and records her deeply moving songs. It is here that Corita, once a nun, became famous as a painter. Here Judith and Milton Stark recently opened Theatre Vanguard, a small, intimate and very special theater where everything unusual is shown in films, theater, dance.

Here Lee Mullican, a painter inspired by American Indian art, created an individual modern expression from this source. He was even given an Indian name. Discovering that woman has a different vision of her body, Mullican's wife, Luchita, paints the female form from a woman's angle, finding new aspects of it.

In *Collages*, my novel about Los Angeles, which came out in 1964, I depicted the independent and adventurous life of Renate Druks, who is now building her second studio home in Malibu. She supervised the workmen so well during a temporary absence of the architect that the workmen presented her with an orange hard hat. She continues her painting, film making, graphic arts. Asked by a group of UCLA students studying *Collages* just how much reality there was in my description of Los Angeles characters, Renate told them that her experience with Raven, who appeared in the book, was very real. She was a girl with long black hair and pale skin who had always wanted a raven and searched until she found one for sale, advertised by a lady in San Francisco. The raven arrived by TWA.

"When she [Raven] found him in his box at the airport he seemed crestfallen and humiliated. His wings were held close to his body as if the flight had handicapped him forever. He looked angrily at the plane as an unworthy rival. He cackled and made harsh angry sounds. Raven took him home.

"She had to buy a huge cage. But she was happy. She felt she had fulfilled a long dream, she felt complete in herself. In the raven lay some mute, unflying part of herself which would now become visible, audible and in flight. His wings, so wide open and power-ful, became her wings. His blackness became her blackness. And the child in Raven who had been too gentle, too docile, now felt liberated of this meek image, felt that the raven had become a part of her she wanted to express, a stronger, darker, more independent self."

When *Collages* was published, the comment of a California student was, "I did not know one could find magic in Los Angeles."

The search for magic is a search for those intent on creating instead of destroying. In the exertion of magic, one discovers many treasures. It only requires faith and a recognition of its appearances.

WALLACE STEGNER

WALLACE STEGNER

THERE WAS A Western Writers Conference in Logan, Utah, that I attended for the purpose of gathering material for the magazine. I flew to Salt Lake City, then changed to a small plane. This lightweight bird carried only six passengers and also made two mail stops en route to Logan. It was my first experience flying so close to the ground, and my stomach needed reassurance that we would not hit bottom before our time.

Utah State was a larger and more beautiful campus than I had expected. The surrounding foliage was lush, and grand old pines lined the walks. We were put up in dorms and assembled at the auditorium for the lectures. Participants talked of fur traders, mountain men, manifest destiny. My particular interest was Wallace Stegner's talk—Western Landscape—a subject I knew little about except to have made the personal observation that the grass was certainly greener in the East. I had read Stegner's novels but was not yet aware of his dedication to the environment. In the 1970s, *ecology* was a comparatively new word and environment and ecology were not the popular concerns that they are today, though we did have some warnings from Richard Lillard in *Eden in Jeopardy* and Rachel Carson in *Silent Spring*.

Stegner stood at the podium, a handsome, white-haired figure. He defined the desert and its aridity with the poetic power that was to win him a Pulitzer Prize. His language created a vision of cacti rooted in the desert, decorated with passionate blooms of color on their prickly, untouchable surfaces. He explained the difference between desert growth and the green, flowering, Eastern counterparts. He analyzed the scheme of nature in its clever plan for indigenous landscapes.

The talk was so vivid that I immediately saw it as an appropriate article for us. After the session, I joined the group who gathered around him. He graciously agreed to meet me later in the day and we talked about the possible publication of his presentation. He had no objection and would check it out with the Logan people concerning rights, etc., but he anticipated no conflict. In the meantime, we walked over to his rooms on campus where his wife, Mary, was patiently relaxing in their quarters while demands were being made on her husband. Then and there, he gave me a copy of the talk so that he wouldn't have to remember to mail it to me. To have it in hand was more than I had hoped for, though we had discussed a fee.

We met again at the end of the conference at a barbecue picnic set in a glen. Logan was a natural wonderland. I gathered pine cones for souvenirs while streams rushed about in the background. I returned home in high spirits feeling like little Jack Horner who had picked out a plum.

We published the article quickly (September, 1972), and I kept trying, greedily, for more. I asked Stegner for an article on some of the young students he had taught at Stanford. But he was a very busy writer. He wrote back in June, 1974:

> Thanks for your letter and the invitation. I can't accept it now. I'm just into a novel, and I rather like it. . . . So I couldn't accept your invitation—for at least a year. But it is possible that after that—note the word possible—that I might want to write a few pieces on such writers as Larry McMurtry, Tom Mayer, Edward Abbey and perhaps others. All three of those I name have been my students and all are good, in different ways. . . . If

you catch me at the right moment with the right proposition I might sing. . . .

I kept trying and he kept "postponing" me for one major project or another. And then, by chance, I learned through L.C. Powell that he had delivered a dedication address at the opening of the University of Arizona library. I wrote him to find out if we could publish his "ready-made article." He wrote back:

> I thought of sending you that speech, since you had been kind enough to ask for something. . . . But then I thought it was pretty solemn for your pages. If you can use it fine. Perhaps you ought to cast your editorial eye over it and tell me what you'd like to see done to it before I make any revisions. My own inclination would be to take the "speech" tone out of it. . . .

I answered:

> I don't think the piece needs much repair. It isn't even too "speechy" except for the opening two sentences and the second paragraph. Then it seems fine until almost the end. Am enclosing a xerox so I can better indicate the section that might need cutting. . . . If you don't agree with these suggestions, please do what you feel comfortable with. . . .

He sent in his revisions—and once again we were happy, temporarily. For me, the "library piece" defined a cultural monument on the Western landscape. In future correspondence he said he was a "frail reed for an editor to lean on." He never said "no" but continued to say "maybe" until I left my post.

■

Thoughts in a Dry Land

BY WALLACE STEGNER

"You have to get over the color green; you have to
quit associating beauty with gardens and lawns;
you have to get used to an inhuman scale."

The western landscape is of the wildest variety and contains every
sort of topography and landform, even most of those familiar from
farther east. Bits of East and Middle West are buried here and there
in the West, but none of the true West is buried in the East. The
West is short-grass plains, alpine mountains, geyser basins, pla-
teaus and mesas and canyons and cliffs, salinas and sinks, sagebrush
and Joshua tree and saguaro deserts. If only by reason of their size,
the forms of things are different, but there is more than mere size to
differentiate them. There is nothing in the East like the granite
horns of Grand Teton or Teewinot, nothing like the volcanic neck
of Devil's Tower, nothing like the travertine terraces of Mammoth
Hot Springs, nothing like the flat crestline and repetitive profile of
the Vermilion Cliffs. You know that these differences are themselves regional—that the West, which stretches from around the
ninety-eighth meridian to the Pacific, and from the forty-ninth
parallel to the Mexican border, is actually half a dozen subregions
as different from one another as the Olympic rain forest is from
Utah's slickrock country, or Seattle from Santa Fe.

You know also that the western landscape is more than topography and landforms, dirt and rock. It is, most fundamentally,
climate—climate which expresses itself not only as landforms but
as atmosphere, flora, fauna. And here, despite all the local variety,
there is a large, abiding simplicity. Not all the West is arid, yet
except at its Pacific edge, aridity surrounds and encompasses it.
Landscape includes such facts as this. It includes and is shaped by
the way continental masses bend ocean currents, by the way the

prevailing winds blow from the West, by the way mountains are pushed up across them to create well-watered coastal or alpine islands, by the way the mountains catch and store the snowpack that makes settled life possible in the dry lowlands, by the way they literally create the dry lowlands by throwing a long rain shadow eastward. Much of the West except the narrow Pacific littoral lies in one or another of those rain shadows such as the Great Basin and lower Colorado River country, or in the semi-arid steppes of the Montana, Dakota, Nebraska, Wyoming, Colorado and New Mexico plains.

Aridity, more than anything else, gives the Western landscape its character. It is aridity that gives the air its special dry clarity; aridity that puts brilliance in the light and polishes and enlarges the stars; aridity that leads the grasses to evolve as bunches rather than as turf; aridity that exposes the pigmentation of the raw earth and limits, almost eliminates, the color of chlorophyll; aridity that erodes the earth in cliffs and badlands rather than in softened and vegetated slopes, that has shaped the characteristically swift and mobile animals of the dry grasslands and the characteristically nocturnal life of the deserts. The West, Walter Webb said, is a semi-desert with a desert heart. If I prefer to think of it as two long chains of mountain ranges with deserts or semi-deserts in their rain shadow, that is not to deny his assertion that the primary unity of the West is a shortage of water.

The consequences of aridity multiply by a kind of domino theory. In the attempt to compensate for nature's lacks we have remade whole sections of the western landscape. The modern West is as surely Lake Mead and Lake Powell and the Fort Peck reservoir, the irrigated greenery of the Salt River Valley and the smog blanket over Phoenix, as it is the high Wind River or the Wasatch or the Grand Canyon. We have acted upon the western landscape with the force of a geological agent. But aridity still calls the tune, directs our tinkering, prevents the healing of our mistakes; and vast unwatered reaches still emphasize the contrast between the desert and the sown. As Professor Webb also said the West is an oasis civilization, something different in profound ways from the civilization east of the line which marks an annual mean rainfall of twenty inches.

Aridity has made a lot of difference in us, too, since Americans first ventured up the Missouri into the unknown in the spring of 1804. Our intentions varied all the way from romantic adventurousness to schemes of settlement and empire; all the way from delight in dehumanized nature to a fear of the land empty of human settlements, monuments, and even history. Let me call your attention to one book that contains most of the possible responses. It is called *The Great Lone Land,* and it is about the Canadian, not the American West, and it was written by an Irish officer in the British army, William F. Butler. But the report out of which the book grew was responsible for the creation of the Royal Northwest Mounted Police, and so had a big hand in the development of western Canada. Butler was also an intelligent observer, a romantic, and a man who loved both wild country and words. He is writing in 1872:

"The old, old maps which the navigators of the sixteenth century framed from the discoveries of Cabot and Cartier, of Varrazanno and Hudson, played strange pranks with the geography of the New World. The coastline, with the estuaries of large rivers, was tolerably accurate; but the center of America was represented as a vast inland sea whose shores stretched far into the Polar North; a sea through which lay the much-coveted passage to the long-sought treasures of the old realms of Cathay. Well, the geographers of that period erred only in the description of ocean which they placed in the central continent, for an ocean there is, and an ocean through which men seek the treasures of Cathay, even in our own times. But the ocean is one of grass, and the shores are the crests of the mountain ranges, and the dark pine forests of sub-Arctic regions. The great ocean itself does not present more infinite variety than does this prairie-ocean of which we speak. In winter, a dazzling surface of purest snow; in early summer, a vast expanse of grass and pale pink roses; in autumn too often a wild sea of raging fire. No ocean or water in the world can vie with its gorgeous sunsets; no solitude can equal the loneliness of a night-shadowed prairie; one feels the stillness, and hears the silence, the wail of the prowling wolf makes the voice of solitude audible, the stars look down through infinite silence upon a silence almost as intense. One saw here the world as it had taken shape and form from the hands of the Creator.''

History builds slowly, starting from scratch, and understanding of a new country depends upon every sort of report, including some that are unreliable, biased, or motivated by personal interest—such a report, say, as Lansford Hastings' *The Emigrant's Guide to Oregon and California.* Across a century and three-quarters since Lewis and Clark pushed off into the Missouri, we have had multitudinous reports on the West—Pike and Long; Catlin and Maximilian of Wied Neuwied; Ashley and Jedediah Smith and Frémont; Bonneville and the Astorians and Nathaniel Wyeth; Spalding and Whitman; the random Oregon and California gold rush diarists; the historians of the compact Mormon migration; the Pacific Railroad Surveys of the 1850s which for many areas were the beginning of precise knowledge; the Powell, Hayden, King and Wheeler surveys and the U.S. Geological Survey that united and continued them. And the dime novels and the Currier and Ives prints; the reports of missionaries and soldiers; the reporters and illustrators for *Leslie's* and *Harper's Weekly;* the painters from Catlin and Miller and Bodmer to Bierstadt and Moran; the photographers from Jackson and Hillers and Haynes and Savage onward; the Fenimore Coopers, Mark Twains, Bret Hartes, Dan de Quilles, Horace Greeleys; the Owen Wisters and Frederic Remingtons; the Andy Adamses and Zane Greys and Eugene Manlove Rhodeses.

True or false, observant or blind, impartial or interested, factual or mythical, it has all gone into the hopper and influenced our understanding and response at least as much as first-hand acquaintance has. But it took a long time. Even learning the basic facts—extents, boundaries, animals, ranges, tribes of men—took a long time. The physical exploration that began with Lewis and Clark was not completed until Almon Thompson led a Powell Survey party into Potato Valley in 1872, and discovered the Escalante River and verified the Henry Mountains, which Powell had seen from a distance on his voyages down the Colorado. The surveying and mapping of great areas of the West was not completed for decades after real exploration had ended; and the trial-and-error (emphasis on the error) by which we began to be an oasis civilization was forced upon us by country and climate, but against the most mule-headed resistance and unwillingness to understand, accept and change.

In the actual desert, and especially among the Mormons where intelligent leadership, community settlement and the habit of cooperation and obedience were present, agricultural adaptation was swift. But in the marginal zone between humid Midwest and semi-arid West it was easy to be deluded, for the difference of just one inch in rainfall, or a slight variation in the seasonal distribution would make the difference between success and failure. And delusion was promoted. The individualism of the frontier, the folklore and habit learned in other regions, the usual politics and boosterism, and land speculation, encouraged settlement on terms sure sooner or later to fail. Cooperation was one lesson the West enforced, and it was learned hard. Bernard DeVoto once caustically remarked, in connection with the myth of western individualism, that the only real individualists in the West had wound up on one end of a rope whose other end was in the hands of a bunch of vigilantes. But a lot of other individualists wound up in the hands of the bank, or trailed back eastward from the dry plains in wagons reading, "In God we trusted, in Kansas we busted," leaving a half-ruined land behind them.

John Wesley Powell submitted his *Reports on the Lands of the Arid Region of the United States, with a More Detailed Account of the Lands of Utah,* on April 1, 1878. That early, partly from studying Mormon, Hispano, and Indian irrigation, he understood and accepted both the fact of aridity and the adaptations that men, institutions, and laws would have to go through if we were ever to settle the West instead of simply raiding and ruining it. He comprehended the symbiotic relationship between highlands and lowlands, he understood rivers as common carriers, like railroads, which should not be encumbered by political boundaries. He knew that the Homestead Act and the rectilinear cadastral surveys that worked in well-watered country would not work in the West, and he advocated a change in the land laws that would limit irrigated farms to eighty acres—all a man needed and all he could work—and enlarge stock farms to four full sections, needed by a small farmer's herd in the way of range. He proposed surveys and political divisions not by arbitrary boundaries but by drainage divides, and he and his pupils and associates virtually created the "Wyoming doctrine" which ties water rights to land.

A revolutionary. He might have saved the West and dust bowls of the 1890s, 1930s and 1950s, as well as the worst consequences of river floods. He might have saved the lives and hopes of all the innocents who put their straddlebugs on dryland homesteads in the Dakotas, Kansas, Nebraska and Montana. But the boosters and the politicians were proclaiming that rain followed the plow; free land and movement westward were ingrained expectations. Habit, politics, and real estate boosterism won out over experience and good sense, and that is part of the history of the West, and of western landscape. Even yet the battle, though to some extent won, is not universally understood. There are historians who grow so incensed over the "myth" of the Great American Desert which began with Pike and Long that they resent the admission of aridity, as well as all "deficiency terminology" in connection with the shortgrass plains.

Ultimately, the settlers of the shortgrass plains learned that water was more important to them than land. They became, by degrees, an oasis civilization and settled down to a relatively thin population because that was what the land would bear.

Karl Frederick Krannzel, in *The Great Plains in Transition,* even suggests that men in the Dakotas and elsewhere had to develop the same mobility that marked the buffalo, antelope, wolves, coyotes and horse Indians in that country. They go as far for a swim or for shopping as an antelope will go for a drink, and for very similar reasons. They often go hundreds of miles to farm. There is a kind of farmer called a suitcase farmer who spends the winter in some town or city, Grand Forks or Bismarck or Minneapolis, but who in early spring hitches his trailer-home to his pickup and takes off for the West—Dakota, Montana or Saskatchewan. There he plants his wheat and works his summer fallow, living through the summer in his trailer and driving forty or fifty miles for his supplies and entertainment. In the fall, he harvests and hauls his crop, does his fall plowing, hitches up his trailer again, and returns to the fleshpots of Bismarck. I know one who goes every winter to San Miguel d'Allende. His alternative would be what the early homesteaders attempted—to make a home out in the desolate plains and live there isolated through the worst winters on the continent. Having lived that life as a boy, I can tell you his mobility, which is as natural as the mobility of the buffalo, is a sensible adaptation.

That is only one sample of how, as we have gone about modifying the western landscape, it has been at work modifying us. And what applies to agricultural and social institutions applies just as surely to our pictorial and literary representations. Perceptions trained in another climate and another landscape have had to be modified. That means we have had to learn to quit depending on perceptual habit. Our first and hardest adaptation was to learn all over again how to see. Our second was to learn to like the new forms and colors and light and scale when we had learned to see them. Our third was to develop new techniques, a new palette, to communicate them. And our fourth, unfortunately out of our control, was to train an audience that would respond to what we wrote or painted.

Years ago I picked up an Iowa aunt of mine in Salt Lake City and drove her down to our cottage on Fish Lake. She was not looking as we drove—she was talking—and she missed the Wasatch, and Mount Nebo, and the Sanpete Valley, and even Sigurd Mountain—the Pahvant—which some people down there call The Big Rock Candy Mountain and which is about as colorful as a peppermint stick. The first thing she really saw, as we turned east at Sigurd, was the towering, level front of the Sevier Plateau above Richfield—level as a rooftree, steep as a cliff, and surging more than a mile straight up above that lush valley. I saw it hit her, and I heard it too, for the talk stopped. I said, "How do you like that, Aunt Min?" for like any Westerner I like to impress Iowans, and the easiest way to do it is with size. She blinked and ruffled up her feathers and assembled herself after the moment of confusion and said, "That's nice. It reminds me of the river bluffs in the county park at Ford Dodge."

She couldn't even see it. She had no experience, no scale, by which to judge an unbroken mountain wall more than a mile high, and her startled mental circuitry could respond with nothing better than the fifty-foot clay banks that her mind had learned to call scenery. She was like the soldiers of Cárdenas, the first white men who ever looked into the Grand Canyon. The river that the Indians had said was half a league wide they judged was about six feet, until they climbed a third of the way down and found that rocks the size of a man grew into things taller than the great tower of Seville, and the six-foot creek, even from four thousand feet above it, was clearly a mighty torrent.

Scale is the first and easiest of the West's lessons. Colors and forms are harder. Easterners are constantly being surprised and somehow offended that California's summer hills are gold, not green. We are creatures shaped by our experiences; we like what we know, more often than we know what we like. To eyes trained on universal chlorophyll, gold or brown hills may look repulsive. Sagebrush is an acquired taste, as are raw earth and alkali flats. The erosional forms of the dry country strike the attention without ringing the bells of appreciation. It is almost pathetic to read the journals of people who came West up the Platte Valley in the 1840s and 1850s and tried to find words for Chimney Rock and Scott's Bluff, and found and clung for dear life to the clichés of castles and silent sentinels.

Listen to Clarence Dutton on the canyon country, whose forms and colors are as far from Hudson River School standards as any in the West:

"The lover of nature, whose perceptions have been trained in the Alps, in Italy, Germany, or New England, in the Appalachians or Cordilleras, in Scotland or Colorado, would enter this strange region with a shock, and dwell there for a time with a sense of oppression, and perhaps with horror. Whatsoever things he had learned to regard as beautiful and noble he would seldom or never see, and whatsoever he might see would appear to him as anything but beautiful and noble. Whatsoever might be bold and striking would at first seem only grotesque. The colors would be the very ones he had learned to shun as tawdry and bizarre. The tones and shades, modest and tender, subdued yet rich, in which his fancy had always taken special delight, would be the ones which are conspicuously absent. But time would bring a gradual change. Some day he would suddenly become conscious that outlines which at first seemed harsh and trivial have grace and meaning; that forms which seemed grotesque are full of dignity; that magnitudes which had added enormity to coarseness have become replete with strength and even majesty; that colors which had been esteemed unrefined, immodest, and glaring, are as expressive, tender, changeful, and capacious of effects as any others. Great innovations, whether in art or literature, in science or in nature, seldom take the world by storm. They must be understood before they can be estimated, and must be cultivated before they can be understood."

Amen. Dutton describes a process of westernization of the perceptions that has to happen before the West is beautiful to us. You have to get over the color green; you have to quit associating beauty with gardens and lawns; you have to get used to an inhuman scale; you have to understand geological time.

Painters of the West have been hunting a new palette for the western landscape from Miller and Bodmer to Georgia O'Keeffe, Maynard Dixon and Millard Sheets. They have been trying to see Western landforms with a clear eye ever since the Baron von Egloffstein, illustrating the report of Lt. Ives, showed the Grand Canyon with rims like puffs of cloud, exaggerated its narrowness and depth, and showed nothing of what the trained eye sees first— the persistence of the level strata and the persistent profile of the cliffs. Writers have been trying to learn how to see, and have been groping for a vocabulary better than castles and silent sentinels, but often amateurs of a scientific bent, such as Dutton, have had to show them how. And audiences, taught partly by direct contact with the landscape and partly by studying its interpreters, have been slowly acquiring a set of perceptual habits and responses appropriate to western forms and colors. Perception, like art and literature, like history, is an artifact, a human creation, and it is not created overnight.

The Westerner is less a person than a continuing adaptation. The West is less a place than a process. And the western landscape that it has taken us a century and three-quarters to learn about, and partially adapt our farming, our social institutions, our laws and our aesthetic perceptions to, has now become our most valuable natural resource, as subject to raid and ruin as the beaver, buffalo, grass, timber and other resources that have suffered from our rapacity. We are in danger of becoming scenery sellers—and scenery is subject to as much enthusiastic overuse and overdevelopment as grass and water. It can lead us into an ill-considered crowding on the heels of our resources. Landscape, with its basis of aridity, is both our peculiar splendor and our peculiar limitation. Without careful controls and restrictions and planning, tourists can be as destructive as locusts—can destroy everything we have learned to love about the West. I include you and me among the tourists, and I include you and me in my warning to entrepreneurs. We should all be forced to file an environmental impact study before we build so much as a privy or a summer cottage, much less a motel, a freeway or a resort.

Sometimes I wonder if Lewis and Clark shouldn't have been made to file an environmental impact study before they started West, and Columbus before he ever sailed. They might never have got their permits. But then we wouldn't have been here to learn from our mistakes, either. I really only want to say that we may love a place and still be dangerous to it. We ought to file that environmental impact study before we undertake anything that exploits or alters or endangers the splendid, spacious, varied, magnificent, and terribly fragile earth that supports us. If we can't find an appropriate government agency with which to file it, we can file it where an Indian would have filed it—with our environmental conscience, our slowly maturing sense that the Earth is indeed our mother, worthy of our love and deserving of our care. That may be the last stage of our adaptation to the western landscape, and it may come too late.

CAREY McWILLIAMS

CAREY McWILLIAMS graduated from the University of Southern California with a law degree. After a trial law stint, he concluded that he could do more for the cause of justice as a journalist than as a lawyer. How right he was. He became a name revered among journalists. He was editor of *The Nation*, a journal of liberal opinion. He was the author of *Factories in the Field*, the story of migratory workers; *Brothers Under the Skin*, an examination of racial minorities; *Southern California: Island on the Land* which documented our cultural landscape, and many other works.

I was in the process of planning the magazine's sixty-fifth birthday. Scanning back issues for possible quotable excerpts, I discovered that McWilliams had been a constant contributor when he lived in California. I wrote him for permission to reprint from one of his pieces. His reply was generous and he indicated that he would, if time permitted, be pleased to consider doing some articles for us in the future. This was an offer I pursued.

I thought up many projects. He did them all: an article on the Irish in California, on writers of the West, impressions on returning to Los Angeles after an absence of many years, a play of history focused on Mexican theater. He had a storage tank of a mind and

Carey McWilliams

he turned out articles that might have taken other journalists months to research, with amazing speed and accuracy. All he needed was a deadline on a subject that interested him and it was met with style and substance. For example, on February 13, 1979, he wrote:

> Since I knew you were in a hurry for this piece I thought I should put all else aside and get to it, even if we are suffering from subzero weather! Do any editing; make any changes. My confidence in your judgment is boundless. Hope the piece meets your needs. Hastily.

When he sent in the story of the influx of the Irish in California for a special Irish issue, I wrote to thank him.

He answered (April 3, 1978):

> Thanks for the nice note; it made my day. I'm glad you have had some favorable comment about the Irish piece; it was fun to write. . . . And I am making notes on the piece about Hollywood writers. Fact is I was in the hospital for six tedious weeks and this has interrupted my schedule as you might imagine. I'm trying hard to finish a book [his autobiography] and want to get it out of the way as soon as possible. You know what interruptions do when you are writing a book. . . . Best ever.

He came to Los Angeles for quick trips now and again—to receive one honor or another—from the *Los Angeles Times* or the ACLU. He attended rehearsals of *Zoot Suit*, a play at the Mark Taper Forum (1979). He had been involved in cooling the Los Angeles zoot suit riots in 1943 when the war tensions ran high and a group of sailors attacked Mexicans wearing zoot suits with "reat pleats." McWilliams, a stalwart friend of minority causes, helped achieve a government directive that temporarily calmed the racist waters.

We would visit on these trips, sometimes only briefly, but with affection. He was accompanied by his lovely, talented novelist wife, Iris. When he came out in 1979 to guest lecture at UCLA, he was coping with cancer. Despite the pain and the discomfort of therapy treatments, he seemed almost to defy his illness with his relentless activity.

In the spring of 1980, I went to New York to visit my daughter, who was then teaching at Columbia. McWilliams lived in the area and we went to see him. Iris warned that he ran out of steam quickly, but wouldn't admit it. We promised not to overstay.

There he was, sitting up in bed, surrounded by books and papers—not letting go—though an odor of death already pervaded the room. He was frail but alert and kept up a lively dialogue. He expressed his horror over nuclear proliferation and the possibility of a Reagan presidency. His sharp mind sliced apart the political scene. He talked about his belief in protest politics—if there is no one to vote for, go with the advocate of exposure. At least the issues will be aired. Then he turned the conversation to the personal. An old friend, novelist John Fante, was on his mind. The last time they had visited, Fante was blind and without a limb as a result of his diabetes. In contrast, Carey tried to make light of his own cancer, when suddenly this no-nonsense man had to stop talking to control the tremor of emotion and quell the tears. The state of the nation held out hope through protest, but his health and that of his sick friend were beyond help. My daughter and I were intensely moved. It was clearly time to leave. We said goodbye and knew it was for the last time.

■

Writers of the Western Shore

BY CAREY McWILLIAMS

When I arrived in Los Angeles, a seventeen-year old migrant from Colorado, in the spring of 1922, I was broke and friendless, a stranger in a strange land. But I had arrived in Los Angeles at the right time: The great boom of the 1920s was well under way and, by good luck, I soon got a job in the business office of the *Los Angeles Times* where my boss, a benevolent despot, made it possible for me to continue my university education while holding down a full-time job.

In those years I was a great Mencken fan and read every book he praised. One day in 1923, while browsing through the stacks at the Los Angeles Public Library, I came across the imposing *Collected Works* of Ambrose Bierce, a writer Mencken particularly admired. Starting with *The Devil's Dictionary* I promptly devoured the twelve volumes and ended up a Bierce addict. I knew that Bierce had lived in California—in fact a Bierce legend of a sort still survived—but that not too much was known about him. So with a self-confidence that in retrospect I find preposterous, I decided to write a book about him. Two years later, *The Argonaut* published the first fruit of this research and, as a result, miraculous things began to happen. I soon had a contract for a book and Mencken had put me in touch with his friend and Bierce's protégé, George Sterling, who opened many doors for me.

It was Sterling who sent Louis Adamic to see me: We met for the first time on September 11, 1926. Louis, who had called to see Sterling at the Bohemian Club, was then employed in the pilot station office located on the breakwater at the entrance to San Pedro harbor. He had been mustered out of the service at San Pedro where there happened to be a small Yugoslav fishing colony. On that first meeting, Louis and I had dinner at Agazzoni's, a long-since forgotten but quite good Italian restaurant on Figueroa Street near Seventh, and talked far into the night. We had many of the same enthusiasms and interests and shared an unappeasable curiosity about Los Angeles and environs. Tall and slender, Louis was high-strung and extremely sensitive but he had a magnificent sense of humor of the robust peasant variety. I have never known anyone whose laughter was more infectious. The two of us were intrigued by the general social and political nuttiness of the 1920s and were determined to capture some of its Southern California manifestations in pieces we wrote for *The American Mercury* and other publications.

After that first meeting, we spent many hours together, junketing about the region, visiting various gurus, prophets and mystics, talking endlessly and laughing most of the time. We had many long talks at the pilot station office in the evenings while Louis was still on duty. It was a beautiful scene as the ships glided in and out of the harbor flashing their mysterious signal lights and, on occasion, with the foghorns booming their sad warnings. Louis usually got off late at night—he liked to work during the day on his writing—so it would often be eleven or twelve o'clock before he could leave. But there was not much he had to do while on duty so the pilot station office, lost in isolation at the end of the breakwater, proved to be a fine place to sit and talk. On weekends he would often visit me in Los Angeles. From our first meeting until he left for New York in 1929, we were incessant companions, exchanging notes, clippings and books. I met his friends: he met mine. We had great fun writing pieces which were published in Haldeman Julius' Little Blue Book series for which we were paid twenty-five dollars a "volume"; but having copies to shower on friends was a special incentive. It was the success of *Dynamite*, his account of class violence, that first brought Louis to national attention.

Shortly before he left for Milford, New Jersey, where he bought a farm, the two of us drove to San Francisco. On the way we detoured to Carmel and late that afternoon I took him around to meet Robinson and Una Jeffers. On this as on previous occasions, Una did most of the talking. Before we left she took us through the slightly ritualized ceremony of inspecting the Irishreed organ in the Hawk Tower, the grove of newly planted trees, and had us gape at the mottoes and legends in Old English that were painted on the beams and panels of Tor House. As usual, Jeffers said very little but he made both of us feel that World War I, about which he seemed to be obsessed, marked the beginning of the end of the kind of civilization we had known. He saw a darker decade looming up ahead in which various forms of Caesarism were likely to emerge. In his eyes, America was a "perishing republic." As we drove up through the pines and cypresses and struck the main highway at Salinas, we talked excitedly about what he had said and what his silences implied. For both of us the visit marked a realization that the world of the 1920s was drawing to a close and would be followed by a period of turbulence and upheaval. Louis promptly proceeded to write a long essay about Jeffers which was published (1929) in the Chapbook Series then being issued by the University of Washington Press under the editorship of Glenn Hughes, while I put my impressions in a piece for *Saturday Night* (August 3, 1929): "Robinson Jeffers: An Antitoxin."

The last time I saw Louis was late in 1950. He and Stella came to visit us at our hilltop home in Elysian Park. Louis seemed extremely tense and ill-at-ease and not at all his old self. He had been working furiously—his self-discipline was always remarkable—and he had seen few of his old friends nor did he want to see them. He did not laugh once which was truly disturbing. Life had suddenly closed in on him. Contrary to what he had resolved should never happen, he had surrendered himself to the passion of politics. He had become a partisan of the Tito regime and its leading spokesman in this country.

In the spring of 1951, we left for New York. Coming out of *The Nation* offices for lunch. I stared, stunned and dismayed, at the headlines: "Louis Adamic Found Shot in Blazing Home." I left immediately for Milford to join Stella. The place was swarming with police and reporters but I had a good, brief talk with Stella. The next day, in a radio interview on WCBS, I tried to put the facts of Louis's life and work, and his tragic death (a possible suicide), in proper perspective.

Two of his books—*Laughing in the Jungle* and *My America*—contain valuable insights about Southern California in the years he spent in the region. But of all his books, I most admire *Grandsons*—he first wanted to call it "A Country Full of Nice People"—which develops his concept of "shadow America" and the problem of identity that seems to plague many Americans. It is dedicated to me and with good reason, for we spent many hours discussing the main theme of the novel and its endless nuances. In fact I wrote a long essay, *Louis Adamic and Shadow America*, which Arthur Whipple, one of Southern California's fine printers of the time, published in book form in a limited edition in 1935. In his books on immigrants and as editor of *Common Ground* from 1940 to 1949. Louis did more to call attention to ethnic values and to dramatize what he called "the secondary consequences" of the immigrant experience than any American of his time. His writings are about due for a rebirth and when, if ever, Henry A. Christian finishes his biography of Louis, that "second reading" or rediscovery will no doubt take place.

One of the magazines published in Los Angeles in the 1920s was *Saturday Night*, edited by Samuel T. Clover, a kindly man with snow-white hair who lived in a lovely old frame house stacked with books, overlooking Echo Park Lake. Clover's career as a journalist in Los Angeles should be researched and documented by some graduate student in search of a good subject for a dissertation. Born in London in 1859, Clover spent a year as an ordinary seaman visiting the South Pacific, an experience which yielded a book of some 200 pages. Later he edited a lively publication in South Dakota, *The Dakota Bell,* and finally came to live in Los Angeles. He was the author of some five novels.

With exceptional patience, Clover encouraged me to flush out writers in Southern California and to contribute pieces about their work for which I was paid at the rate of fifteen dollars an article. In the late 1920s I contributed pieces about Louis Adamic; Jake Zeitlin; Upton Sinclair; Edith Summers Kelley; Jim Tully; Hildegarde Flanner, my favorite California poet; Henry Chester Tracy; Leroy MacLeod, who worked in an ad agency and wrote nostalgic novels about the Middle West (*The Years of Peace, Three Steeples*); J. William Lloyd, the naturalist and friend of Havelock Ellis, who lived in a cabin in the foothills near Burbank called The Swallow's Nest; Roy Milton Iliff, another ad agency novelist (*In the Red*), and other writers. Edith Summers Kelley, of Point Loma, was the author of a fine novel, *Weeds*,—first published in 1923, it was reissued in 1972—and the manuscript of another novel, about Imperial Valley, *The Devil's Hand,* was finally published in 1974. I also wrote about other California writers I had come to know: George Sterling; Gertrude Atherton; Colonel Charles Erskine Scott Wood, who lived in a beautiful villa overlooking the Santa Clara Valley; his wife, Sara Bard Field, the poet; Marie de L. Welch, a fine poet; Idwal Jones; Clarkson Crane, and others. When at his villa, Colonel Wood dressed in the toga of a Roman senator, complete with sandals, and reminded me and others of Zeus, with his long white hair and beard. Beautiful and charming, Sara Bard Field often appeared at The Cats in flowing robes and veils. In the last years of Prohibition, they had a splendid well-stocked wine cellar and were superb hosts.

As part of my coverage of Southern California's rather skimpy literary scene for *Saturday Night*, I met Jake Zeitlin, a young poet from Texas, shortly after his arrival in Los Angeles in 1925, and did a piece about him in November 1927. Jake was then living in a charming hideaway bungalow in Elysian Park and eked out a meager livelihood by peddling rare books. At that first meeting we became and have remained great friends, associated in numberless literary ventures. Later I helped him organize the first of several bookstores. At the Sign of the Grasshopper, near the newly constructed public library, and also his later shop around the corner on West Sixth Street, designed by Lloyd Wright. By stages Jake moved west with the expansion of the city to a place near Westlake Park and, finally, to the famous Red Barn on La Cienega. You never knew just who you might meet in Jake's shops: Aldous Huxley, Hugh Walpole, Edward Weston, Frieda Lawrence, or some young poet who had just hitchhiked his way to Los Angeles. At Jake's prompting, some of us organized Primavera Press which, over the years, published some first-rate books in handsome editions. It was also at Jake's initiative that a group of intellectuals of the period published for a time an interesting and lively "little" magazine, *Opinion* (October 1929 to May 1930). Phil Townsend Hanna, Ward Ritchie, Lawrence Clark Powell, Grace Marian Brown, Arthur Miller, Hildegarde Flanner, Herbert Klein, Lloyd Wright, Jose Rodriquez and others were, as I recall, participants. We used to meet for dinner at René & Jean's French restaurant on West Sixth Street, near Jake's bookshop, but the irreverent talk and gossip always got in the way of getting out the next issue.

One of my close friends of this period was Duncan Aikman who had covered the Harding-Cox presidential campaign for the *New York World* but who later, for reasons of health, joined the editorial staff of a paper in El Paso, and finally came on to Los Angeles to serve as West Coast correspondent for the *Baltimore Sun*. Dunc loved a good time, was not averse to taking a drink, had a highly cultivated sense of humor and a rare talent for inducing pompous politicians to make fools of themselves in interviews. On one occasion the two of us got quite tight and, around midnight, I listened in wonderment and disbelief as Dunc dictated in not bad iambic pentameter a ribald dispatch to the *Sun* about the latest of Aimee Semple McPherson's capers. I often wondered what the night staff of the *Sun* was able to make of that dispatch. I usually trailed along when Dunc interviewed such visiting celebrities as Bertrand Russell and Paul Elmer More. For a brief time, Robert W. Kenny and his friend Roy Allen published a little news weekly in Los Angeles called *Midweek* (1933-1934) which was largely written by Aikman.

At about the same time I met Jake Zeitlin, I also met Stanley Rose, another Texas transplant. A country boy from Matador, Texas, Stanley had run away from home to enlist in the army in World War I, telling the recruiting officers that he understood they were looking for machine gunners. At war's end he and a friend both of whom had been wounded, feigned mysterious psychiatric disorders and thereby managed to spend a year or more in a delightful facility near Stanford University. There Stanley acquired a taste for reading and a fondness for books. When the authorities finally caught on to the ruse and booted them out. Stanley came to Los Angeles where he, too, peddled books for a time, primarily risqué items which he hawked in the studios. I first met him shortly after he had opened a small shop off Hollywood Boulevard a few blocks east of Vine. I lent Stanley a hand in organizing the two stores he later opened, the first on Vine near Hollywood Boulevard and the other next to Musso & Frank's. Both were favorite meeting places for writers: Bill Saroyan, George Milburn, Erskine Caldwell, Louis Adamic, William Faulkner, Nathanael West, Frank Fenton, John Fante, Jo Pagano, John Bright, Jim Tully, Owen Francis, A.I. Bezzerides and others. I first met Saroyan there shortly after he had published a much-discussed essay in *The American Mercury* ostensibly about aspirin and the NRA but really about Saroyan. Stanley's bookstores were for years favorite hangouts for

Hollywood intellectuals, in much the same way that Jake's shops were in downtown Los Angeles. But Jake drew most of the swells and big names, whereas Stanley's stores served as clubhouses for garrulous wise guys and writers on their way up.

Stanley was a superb storyteller and a very funny man whose generosity was proverbial. In the later afternoons, as he began to warm up with a few drinks, he would hold court, entertaining whoever happened to drop in; the performance would invariably continue into early morning hours in the backroom at Musso's. At one time Stanley had been part owner of the Satyr Book Shop on Vine Street. But his two associates in this enterprise managed to induce him to take the rap for a pornographic item which the three of them had published in violation of the copyright. The two associates were married; Stanley was not. So with little difficulty they convinced him that he should assume sole responsibility and glibly assured him that a jail sentence would not be imposed. Always amiable, Stanley entered a plea of guilty, drew sixty days in the cooler, and promptly sent for me. I found him cursing like a pirate in the visitor's room at the Hall of Justice: he had just learned that his two associates had taken over control of the corporation. I arranged to secure his release and we then induced the two associates to buy out his interest. Along with one or two other friends, I then helped him organize the bookstore on Vine Street directly opposite the Satyr Shop.

After a few drinks, Stanley would now and then emerge from the store and, to the vast amusement of his customers, swagger to the curb, shake his fist at his two former associates across the street, and hurl eloquent Texas curses at them. Uneducated but of immense native charm, Stanley was forever being lured on expensive hunting and fishing trips by wealthy actors, writers and directors on their promises to buy large libraries of books, which of course they never did; they merely wanted him along as a court jester. Stanley dressed like a Hollywood swell, spoke like the Texas farm boy he never ceased to be, and carried on as Hollywood's unrivaled entertainer and easiest touch until his death in 1954. We were good friends during all the years he held court in the book stores which have long since become part of the legend of Hollywood.

One of my close friends of the late 1930s and early 1940s was Humphrey Cobb. I knew Humphrey from the time he came to work in Hollywood—at different times at M-G-M, Warner Brothers, Goldwyn and Paramount—until his death in 1944. He came to Hollywood shortly after *Paths of Glory* was published in June 1935. Based on an actual incident in World War I (reported in the *New York Times* of July 2, 1934), it became an immediate best seller, was adapted to the stage by Sidney Howard but closed after five or six performances. In 1957 it was produced as a movie by Stanley Kubrick; in fact it was his first film production. Humphrey had falsified his age in order to enlist in the Royal Montreal regiment of the First Canadian Division at the outset of World War I and had seen some violent action in France. A small feisty man with closely cropped hair, his speech clipped and tart, he was amusingly irascible and never suffered fools gladly. Nor was he ever known to walk away from an argument.

When I first met him he was recovering from a heart attack and worked mostly at home, first in Brentwood, later in Flintridge. He hated the atmosphere of the studios and had little interest in films. As the international situation began to heat up in the late 1930s, he became so obsessed with what was happening that he could think or talk of little else. Hating war as he did—*Paths of Glory* is one of the strongest indictments of militarism written in our time—he was nevertheless outraged at the failure of world opinion to check fascist aggression; in fact he could hardly wait for the next war to start. Concerned about his health, Anne Louise, his wife, asked me to visit him as often as possible since he seemed to be less agitated when he talked politics with me than with some of his other friends. So I made a point of spending as much time with him as I could, particularly when the various crises crested, and now and then would bring friends along to help relieve the tension. During the Munich crisis Louis Adamic and I sat up most of the night with Cobb listening to short-wave radio broadcasts. The next day he wrote a magnificent letter to Neville Chamberlain, renouncing the dual British citizenship he had acquired by service in the Canadian Army and returning a handful of decorations. After Pearl Harbor he returned to New York to work with the

O.W.I. (Writers War Board), and I saw him there from time to time until his death.

Hans Otto Storm, another writer of that period, wrote some novels that deserve more attention than they have ever received. Storm was born in California and grew up in Anaheim. He is said to have been the first American to die in World War II. His novels *Full Measure, Made in the U.S.A., Count Ten* and *Pity the Tyrant* should be remembered: of these the last is my favorite. Frank Fenton I also knew quite well. Between screen assignments he wrote two novels, *A Place in the Sun* and *Which Way My Journey Lies*. Better than most novels of the period, the first captures significant aspects of the Southern California scene. Once Frank, to my total astonishment, delivered to me a book-length manuscript in blank verse and sought my aid in finding a publisher for it; none, of course, was found. A cynic's cynic, Frank knew the world of the studios very well; he often boasted that he had not been east of Vine Street in all the years he lived in Los Angeles. A.I. Bezzerides was another writer I came to know in those years; his best known novel is *The Long Haul*, a novel about wildcat truckers which was later made into a movie. Before his first novel was published, he used to come to my office to talk out wonderful novels, complete with plot, character, setting. I never ceased to marvel at his ability to recite with enthusiasm a detailed outline of an entire novel to an audience of one person.

One day I got a letter from Mencken saying that a promising young writer whose first story had just been published in *The American Mercury* wanted to meet me. His name was John Fante. So I asked him to have lunch—the first of countless meetings, at all hours, in every conceivable setting and circumstance. The visitor was a young Italian-American, quite short, with wicked rolling black Italian eyes and a glorious sense of humor. Like me a Coloradoan, he had come to live in Wilmington in 1930 where he worked for a time in a fish cannery. Later he spent a year at Long Beach City College where he wrote his first published story, "Altar Boy." When the March 1933 earthquake struck he was spending a flirtatious evening with one of the more attractive young instructresses at the college—no doubt discussing Chaucer, Spenser,

Shakespeare and other subjects of high literary import. But with the first terrifying tremors, he abandoned the teacher and lit out for Roseville, California, where his parents then lived, and never stopped until he got there. To this day John shudders at the thought of earthquakes.

The day after he first called, I was surprised to note that he had been interviewed by a reporter for the *Los Angeles Examiner;* an accompanying photograph showed him with rolled up sleeves and apron serving as a busboy in a saloon-and-restaurant on West Third, a few doors from Hill Street. There he had become an overnight celebrity who was asked to autograph menus and copies of the *Mercury* containing his first published story. Beaming on the beaming busboy was a beaming waitress who seemed even more delighted with his success than the author. It was indeed a happy time for John, who lived on Bunker Hill, made five dollars a week plus meals, and wrote admirable short stories. Those who wrote him fan letters received a formal printed acknowledgment which said that Mr. Fante had been so overwhelmed with similar mail that personal responses were out of the question. In the *Examiner* interview he said that he had been encouraged to seek a career as a writer by H. L. Mencken and Carey McWilliams. I was delighted to find myself listed as a sponsor on such brief acquaintance. From our first meeting until I left for New York in 1951 to edit *The Nation,* I spent many hours with John. He once dedicated a book to me as a "good friend but evil companion." I can say the same of him, in spades; he was, indeed, a more deplorable influence on me than I ever was on him. Of his novels, *Wait Until Spring; Bandini; Ask the Dust; Full of Life* (made into a movie with Judy Holliday); and *The Brotherhood of the Grape, Ask the Dust* is my favorite; it provides a finely-etched view of the underside of the Los Angeles scene of the period.

I had long had many Filipino friends in California because of my interest in their problems. In this way I came to know Carlos Bulosan who more sensitively than any of his countrymen recorded their often unhappy experience in the United States. A frail, almost childlike person, Carlos came to this country in 1930 at the age of seventeen from his father's small farm in Luzon, in the central

Philippines, with only three years of schooling and very little English. He never returned to the islands and never became an American citizen. He often came to see me and I would introduce him to various friends, including John Fante, who was one of the first American novelists to write perceptively about Filipinos, as in his story, "Helen, Thy Beauty." For some years in the late 1940s, Carlos usually spent Christmas and New Year's Eve with the Fantes, John and Joyce, and on most of these festive occasions Iris and I were present. He began to write during a long confinement in the Los Angeles County Hospital with a collapsed lung but his first short story was published when he was working in a fish cannery in San Pedro. Some of his stories were included in O'Brien's *Best American Story* collections. During the war, Stephen Vincent Benét, Will Durant and Booth Tarkington were asked to contribute articles to the *Saturday Evening Post* on three of the four freedoms; at Louis Adamic's suggestion, Carlos wrote the fourth on "freedom from hunger." A countryman once warned Carlos that it was "hard to be a Filipino in California," as indeed it was in the 1930s; "I came to know afterwards," he wrote, "that in many ways it was a crime to be a Filipino in California." But he never entirely lost faith in this country: "Somewhere there is a star for me. Wait for me, star of hope!" *America is in the Heart* is, as one Filipino critic has said, 30 percent autobiographical, 50 percent case history, and 20 percent pure fiction, but for all that it remains a social classic: the best reflection of the Filipino immigrant experience. Carlos died in Seattle, in December 1956, at age forty-one.

John Fante has written one of the best descriptions of what Carlos was like as a person:

"A tiny person with a limp, with an exquisite face, almost facially beautiful, with gleaming teeth and lovely brown eyes, shy, generous, terribly poor, terribly exiled in California, adoring Caucasian women, sartorially exquisite, always laughing through a face that masked tragedy, a Filipino patriot, a touch of the melodramatic about him, given to telling wildly improbable stories about himself, disappearing from Southern California for months at a time, probably to work in a Seattle or Alaska cannery, showing up finally at my home with some touching gift, a book of poems, a box of Filipino candy.... If I were a good Christian I think I might label him a saint, for he radiated kindness and gentleness."

A miraculous place, the western shore, and a constant challenge to writers. "Here," Hildegarde Flanner once wrote, "is a centering of human energy and desire.... It may be the quality of life has here more of future and hope and excitement, as well as more uncertainty, than in some communities long settled and not constantly changing. In any case, one is more aware, above the exploitation and commercialization, that here human energy and purpose, having reached the limits of physical advance, are bound to flow back upon themselves and in doing so must either stagnate or create."

■

And the People Came

I'm going to California,
The gold dust for to see ...
Oh! Suzanna.

BY CAREY McWILLIAMS

Any listing of major historical happenings between the centennial and the bicentennial must include the phenomenal upsurge of population in California. It represents, indeed, one of the great migrations of modern times. To be sure, it began in the 1850s with the discovery of gold, itself a major event in American history. But it was only after the centennial that California began to grow as no other state has grown. It took some 200 years to settle the eastern seaboard states with sufficient firmness to permit the big push westward into the Mississippi Valley, but only a century—thanks to the "discovery" of California—to complete the pattern of national settlement. By 1850 the area of settlement had been extended to the banks of the Mississippi and then suddenly, and rather unexpectedly, California emerged as a lodestar, a powerful magnet, that drew population westward at a steadily accelerating clip.

Two intertwined events set the stage: the war with Mexico and the discovery of gold. Of the war with Mexico, at the conclusion of which we acquired 55 percent of the land area of Mexico (including Texas), the historian Don E. Fehrenbacher has said that California was "the heart of the matter . . . the gleam in President James Polk's eye." Polk and his advisors thought we should seize that vast expanse of thinly settled territory before Britain or some other power moved in. But neither he nor his advisors could have anticipated the speed and magnitude of the migration movement their actions set in motion. Three dates tell the story: January 24, 1848, when gold was discovered; February 2, 1848, when the Treaty of Guadalupe Hidalgo was signed; and December 1848, when President Polk told the nation there was "an abundance of gold in California"—which by then was not news.

In January 1963, Governor Edmund Brown proclaimed a four-day holiday by way of celebrating the fact that California had become the most populous state. The observances should have been national for migration to California, from the beginning, has had major national significance. It has been an experience "without parallel anywhere else in the United States or in the world, in volume, velocity, scope, continuity and variety," said Moses Rischin in *California History Reconsidered*.

Between 1900 and 1970 the state's population grew by a figure virtually equal to the total national increment gained by migration for the entire nineteenth century. In the decade 1950-60 new migrants were arriving at an estimated rate of 1,600 a day—a century after the discovery of gold. Over a dozen decades, California's population doubled roughly every twenty years. The implications have been far-ranging but, as I wrote quite some years ago, "the single most distinctive fact about the culture of California has been the perpetually high proportion of newly arrived residents among its inhabitants." While the ratio of native-born has been increasing, the statement still holds. In 1960, 43 percent of the population had been born in California (a figure that includes children born of immigrant parents); by 1970 the estimate had risen to 47.4 percent which still gives numerical ascendance to those born elsewhere.

Immigration and migration have been twin aspects of our national history from the outset but California has always been a special case. Migrants from almost every point on the compass— China, Australia, Latin America, Europe—set out for California with news of the discovery of gold. Only Africa and the Middle East failed to send visible contingents. Unlike most migration movements, the earliest migrants to California often traveled the greatest distances. In the period from 1860 to 1880, Chinese constituted roughly a fourth of all immigrants to the state. In a manner of speaking, there were hardly any natives on hand to greet the early migrants. In 1860 residents born in other states outnumbered natives in the ratio of two to one. In that year, by one estimate, the foreign-born constituted 38.6 percent of the population—a remarkably high percentage for a "pioneer" state. As late as 1870 the foreign-born outnumbered California residents born in other states but after 1920 the latter took a commanding four-to-one lead. A high percentage of Californians have always lived in urban areas; San Francisco, it has been said, is the one great city that was never a village. In 1890 the state's population was classified as 41 percent urban; today 90 percent would be a reasonable estimate. So it is not surprising that a high percentage of the foreign-born live in urban communities. In 1960, according to Rischin, 30 percent of the San Francisco-Oakland metropolitan region was made up of foreign stock deriving from eighty-four countries. But of more significance perhaps is the fact that foreign-born have long been unusually well represented in rural areas. Nor has California lost its attraction for the foreign-born. In 1940 New York still had more aliens but by 1960 California had moved ahead and by 1970 it accounted for 22 percent of all registered aliens. From earliest times, it has attracted more migrants from Mexico and Asia than the other states.

The presence of such a cosmopolitan population has had important economic consequences. Even in the 1850s the population was sufficiently cosmopolitan to enable it to respond to the diverse opportunities implicit in what was and still is an unusual physical and economic environment. The story of Agoston Haraszthy, the Hungarian immigrant who did so much to establish California as a major wine-producing province, is merely one of many that might be cited to demonstrate the state's enormous indebtedness to the foreign-born. Among other groups, Italians, Armenians, Azoreans, Danes, Basques, Chinese, Filipinos, Japanese, Hindus, Yugoslavs, the so-called Volga Germans and, most emphatically, the Spanish-speaking, have made valuable contributions to the culture of the state and its economic development. In the years (1934-39) when I contributed a regular monthly section—"Tides West"—to this publication, I had occasion again and again to call attention to what the presence of these various ethnic groups had meant in terms of the state's rapid economic development and its ability to exploit a variety of resources with which the native-born were not familiar.

Two examples may suggest the fascinating social history to be tapped in the experience of these various ethnic groups. Californians have a notion that many Portuguese reside in the state, but perhaps not more than 5 percent trace their ancestry to mainland Portugal and another 5 percent to the island of Madeira. The rest of California's "Portuguese" turn out to be Azoreans. According to news reports, more Azoreans are living in California today (350,000) than in the Azores (300,000). Since the 1970 census lists 35,418 as foreign-born, most of them are now subsumed in the native-born category. While the first Azoreans came to the state in the 1890s as sailors and fishermen, most of them are now concentrated in the dairy industry, in such communities as Tulare, Hanford, Tipton, Pixley, Los Baños, Chowchilla, Mendota and Firebaugh. Two Azoreans, incidentally, have served in the state legislature. Of equal interest and importance are the large Basque colonies in Fresno and Bakersfield. Basques have made prodigious contributions to the state's sheep and wool industries. Today most of an estimated 50,000 Americans of Basque descent reside in

California and Nevada (U.S. Senator Paul Laxalt of Nevada is of Basque parentage). Each year several hundred Basque sheepherders are flown to Bakersfield from their homes in the Pyrenees. Given one- or two-year contracts, each of these recruited workers is responsible for a block of 1,500 to 2,000 sheep. In some years as many as 75,000 sheep are driven, in this manner, along the 400-mile, century-old sheep trail that extends from the west end of Kern County to Bodie, near Mono Lake.

In important respects the early migration to California was unlike the movement that spread through the Middle West from the eastern seaboard states. For one thing it was largely made up of men without families. Many—perhaps most—did not think of themselves as pioneers or settlers. Jeffrey Paul Chan has written that the Chinese, for example, "never wanted to be pioneers." Bancroft bitterly and a bit unfairly said of the first arrivals that they "came for gold and nothing else. . . . Their achievement was a hole and they did not even stop to fill it up when they hurried away to make another hole elsewhere. Such was pioneering on the gold-bitten coast." Bancroft to the contrary, however, many of those who came to California to pan for gold did stay on, notably in the smaller Northern California communities. But it is true that California was never a typical pioneer state.

Most of the first native-born immigrants came not from the Middle West but from the eastern seaboard. In 1860 two-thirds had come from New England, the middle Atlantic and east north-central states, and New York. From 1860 to 1900, New York was the leading source of immigration. Ocean transportation was no doubt a factor: "round the Horn" or across the isthmus. But as the population center of gravity moved westward, more native-born migrants came from midwestern states. Not surprisingly, therefore, Illinois took first place from New York as a source of migrants in 1910 and held the lead until 1940. Since then—particularly since 1950—Texas has been a key state, in large part because the Spanish-speaking have shown an increasing tendency to move to California.

Special factors stimulated the exodus from midwestern farm

states. One dollar excursion fares, once the rail lines had been completed to Southern California, proved to be a nearly irresistible attraction. Many of these migrants had reached or were approaching retirement age and Southern California's fabled warmth and sunshine had a strong appeal to those who had been frostbitten far too long and once too often. The state society, a unique phenomenon, which began to appear in Southern California as early as the 1880s, provides a good indication of the relative importance of the various states-of-origin. As might be expected, the age level in some Los Angeles Basin communities was, for some decades, from 20 to 40 percent above the national average but it has since fallen.

These first migrants from farms and small towns in the Middle West were not sybarites by any means but they did seek a measure of ease and comfort after years of hard work and slight exposure to the amenities. And they had, in many cases, substantial means. But not all of them found what they sought. For as Rischin points out, the strains of migration often exacted a steep price; membership in a state society is no substitute for severed personal, family, religious, social and community ties. Divorce and suicide rates twice the national average—for certain periods—suggest the degree of loneliness some migrants experienced. At one time, San Diego, today such a joyous city, was known as "the jumping off place"; it had the highest suicide rate in the country, as I helped Edmund Wilson document in one of the chapters of his book *The American Jitters*. In this respect, migration to California has been a special case for two reasons: Most migrants, native or foreign-born, have traveled considerable distances in coming to California. For most migrants—and notably so in the early decades—it was a jump, a quantum leap. Also the new environment was for many radically different from their native habitats. Over the years the shock of transition has abated with improved transportation, better communications, and more mature west coast communities but there can be little doubt that for many migrants the move entailed, as Rischin puts it, "radical upheaval and psychological displacement." On the other hand, there has been little evidence of any large-scale movements back to the states of origin, which would indicate that if migrants have not always found what they sought they have been reasonably satisfied with what they found. As to regions of origin, the 1970 census gives the following breakdown for native-born Americans now residing in California: northeast, 1,348,109; north central, 3,146,783; South, 2,437,080; west, 1,494,885.

Not only has California always had a high proportion of foreign-born, with many ethnic groups represented, but its population has a special racial mix. The aboriginal California cultural area once contained from 120,000 to 150,000 Indians who spoke some 21 different languages and 138 separate dialects. By 1900 no more than 15,000 Indians were left in the state. But by 1960 the number had risen to 36,000 and by 1970 to 88,271, the latter increase being due in large part to an influx of reservation Indians to the Los Angeles area. The Indian experience—like so many other aspects of California's social history—was a special case if only because there were few real tribes; Indians were about as heterogeneous as other Californians. Using current estimates add: 212,121 persons of Japanese descent, 170,374 Chinese, 148,154 Filipinos, 16,684 Koreans, 1,397,138 Negroes, and 3,101,584 Spanish-speaking. The Korean total is considerably larger than this estimate indicates. A change in immigration quotas in 1965 brought as many as 200,000 to this country. Some moved on to New York and other areas but 45,000 have settled in the Los Angeles area of recent years. At one time Filipinos seemed to be a disappearing California minority. Mostly aging single men, lonely, discouraged, many ill or crippled, it was thought they would take advantage of the Repatriation Act and return to the Philippines which had been granted independence. But the 1965 changes in immigration regulations brought a new influx: Filipino immigration jumped from 2,545 in that year to 25,471 in 1970. Since then about 20,000 have entered every year; San Francisco has today a Filipino community of more than 20,000 (said to be its fastest growing racial minority) and there is a large backlog of applications for visas. The new Filipino immigrants include many college graduates: doctors, engineers, teachers, nurses and other professionals.

The percentage of native-born among the Japanese and Chinese minorities is increasing; even so new immigration quotas have added to the totals for both groups. Under the old quota system Chinese immigrants were restricted to about 200 a year. Now some 8,000 enter the port of San Francisco each year, most of them from Hong Kong, a few from Taiwan. Chinatown, as might be expected, is overflowing; today some 35,000 Chinese-Americans reside in other neighborhoods and communities in the Bay Area. In addition to new immigrants from Japan, California has also doubtless received its share of a 1960 estimate of 25,000 Japanese war brides. Also sizable colonies of Samoans can be found in the state today. "Americanization" has disrupted the culture and economy of American Samoa and some 60,000 Samoans are reported to have left for Hawaii and the West Coast. As U.S. nationals American Samoans have free entry and can become citizens. Micronesia may also contribute to this migration once its status is finally determined. Also a number of native Hawaiians, of mixed stock, now live in California (4,634 in Los Angeles County in 1972). More recently Vietnamese refugees have established a foothold. Some 10,000 have settled in San Diego County and the first Vietnamese Buddhist temple was dedicated in Los Angeles on January 13. The Asian immigrant influence is, therefore, almost certain to be more pronounced in the future than it has been in the past. Asian cultural influences extend back to the Gold Rush period and a younger generation of Asian-Americans is mining this field of research with diligence and enthusiasm. Publications such as the *Yardbook Reader* (Vol. III, 1974) and studies in the *Bulletin of Concerned Asian Scholars* are shedding a new light on neglected aspects of Asian culture influences. Today Sadakichi Hartmann, Carlos Bulosan and other writers identified with California are being read with a new interest just as the work of Asian artists identified with California—Taro Yashima and Mine Okubo among others—is receiving the same attention.

Blacks have long fared somewhat better in California than in other non-southern states if only because the dominant prejudice, in times past, has been directed against Orientals and Mexican-Americans. Even so, blacks did not show much interest in California until World War II; since then their numbers have shown a sharp increase. World War II also affected the status of Chinese and Japanese. Although the Japanese suffered severe economic losses from the constitutionally indefensible wartime mass evacuation program, it jarred them into a new political awareness and concern for civil rights. The way in which Japanese-Americans rallied, on their own initiative, to the defense of Dr. Thomas Noguchi, chief medical examiner-coroner of Los Angeles County, against whom some spurious charges had been filed, is merely one indication of the passing of "the old order" among Japanese residents. Another example is the way in which sansei or third generation students defied their nisei parents and issei grandparents by tending to side with blacks and Chicanos in the controversy involving Dr. S.I. Hayakawa at San Francisco State College. Similarly World War II marked the emergence of new attitudes among resident Chinese-Americans. Among the oldest California racial minority, Chinese-Americans have been the last to be heard in the struggle for independence and fairer treatment but they have been making up for lost time. California once had, as we all know, a strong "nativist" movement, largely directed against Orientals, heavily backed by organized labor, which for nearly fifty years was a dominant force in state politics. Today its force is largely spent. In fact developments since World War II tend to confirm Dr. Robert Park's optimistic view of California as a "racial frontier" which would, he thought, ultimately set a new standard of better racial understanding and acceptance. At the height of the "nativist" agitation, California was projected as "the last asylum of the native born"; it has proven to be anything but that.

It is virtually impossible to be precise about the numbers of Spanish-speaking in California. The 1970 census gave a total of 3,101,509 in the Spanish language and surname categories, of whom 654,481 were listed as foreign-born. But these estimates are unreliable. The number of foreign-born fluctuates constantly as does the number of "illegal" aliens. On June 10, 1970, the *Los Angeles Times* bravely ventured a guess that there were between "100,000 and 200,000" illegal Mexican aliens in the county. The vagueness of the estimate indicates the nature of the problem. The 1,600-mile border with Mexico has never been, and probably never will be, effectively policed. Neither the language nor the surname test is entirely reliable. For example there are many Chileans in California with German names. Incidentally there is a sizable colony of Cubans—perhaps 50,000—most of whom live in San Francisco. All that can be said is that the Spanish-speaking constitute the largest ethnic minority in the state and one that is certain to increase in size and influence. In less than twenty years Los Angeles County may have 2.9 million; indeed the Spanish-speaking may well outnumber other "whites" in the city of Los Angeles by 1990. By then, it has been estimated, the Spanish-speaking and blacks (expected by that date to total 1.5 million in Los Angeles County) would alone account for 50.58 percent of the county's population. The Spanish-speaking thus stand an excellent chance of reacquiring a strong position in what was once a Mexican outpost. Nor do numbers alone suggest their potential influence. The Hispanic imprint is on the land, reflected in its place names, speech, architecture and, increasingly, in the arts. The fascinating murals to be seen on the walls of housing projects and other buildings in East Los Angeles are harbingers of a growing Chicano awareness and cultural maturity.

What brought these teeming millions of migrants to California in little more than a century? The "pull" factors—attractions and opportunities—have been paramount. It is an oft-told tale: gold, wheat (the ocean-going trade with Liverpool merchants: in 1881-82 California wheat filled the holds of 500 ships in San Francisco's harbor), cattle and sheep, wine, a wide range of fruit and vegetable crops after the introduction of the refrigerator car in the 1880s, cotton, oil, tourism, motion pictures, expanding service industries and a huge increase in federal spending: between 1940 and 1970, $100 billion in federal dollars was spent in California—more than in any other state—most of it in aerospace and related fields. I would emphasize some intangible factors in addition, such as California's magic worldwide image, which has existed since the name first appeared on maps as an exotic subtropical island (and indeed it *is* a kind of island), an image which became indelibly etched in the world's imagination with the discovery of gold. I would also stress the amazing range of its resources—the 300 or more crops—and the attraction of the wide range of life-styles made possible by its climate, resources and culture, including the mix of its population. The impoverished Joads came west because they had been tractored off the land, but even they knew that beyond the desert and the last mountain range was Eden, a promised land of milk, honey and jobs.

Rapid and continuous growth has dimmed California's attractions to some extent—its image is not as bright as it once was—and ecologists and concerned citizens have combined in an effort to check improvident growth and reckless expansion. Beginning noticeably in the 1960s, many Californians became increasingly distressed by the brutalization of the environment and began to question the equation that more people necessarily means more jobs and more jobs more people. But the population will increase for the immediate future at an estimated rate of 2-3 percent by contrast with a 7 percent annual increase of not so many years back. Demographers foresee perhaps 30,000,000 residents by 1980, 40,000,000 by the year 2000.

The explosion of California—and it has been that—must rank as a major historical happening of the period between 1876 and 1976. It made possible a new American relationship with the countries around the rim of the Pacific. It provided an indispensable link in the chain of expansion by which Hawaii and Alaska were acquired. The energies it released have flowed steadily eastward in the form of new products, new wealth, new practices, new crops, new relationships, new ways of doing things, new patterns of living. It has shifted the balance of economic and political power in the nation and is a key factor in the much-publicized emergence of the "sun belt" states. In bicentennial terms what it represents is an exciting reenactment, in a new and brilliant setting, of the original drama of settlement—the movement of many peoples into a new land—staged with a cast in which Orientals and Spanish-speaking have figured more prominently than in the original version. Act I, settlement of the eastern seaboard states; Act II, the westward march to the banks of the Mississippi; Act III, the "discovery" of California.

Over the years orators and historians—some of whom tend to be oracular—have often and fondly indulged in rhetorical flourishes and imaginative musings about the new world emerging around the rim of the Pacific, admittedly a great theme. Example: William Henry Seward, ''The Pacific Ocean, its shores, its islands, and the vast regions beyond will become the chief theater of the world in the world's great hereafter.'' Example: Frederick Jackson Turner, ''The age of the Pacific begins, mysterious and unfathomable in its meaning for the future.'' But despite the rise of modern Japan, the Chinese Revolution, two world wars, the Korean War, and the Vietnam War, this mysterious world of the Pacific has yet to emerge in all its potential fullness, force and variety—it remains mysterious and unfathomable. As part of the world that is gradually taking form around the rim of the Pacific, California may well be ''the chief theater'' in the region's ''great hereafter'' which is yet to be.

Jack Smith

I INHERITED JACK SMITH (or as he later put it, he inherited me) from the previous editors. Admitting to a tint of
sexism, he wasn't sure, at first, how it would be to work for a
woman editor. He didn't express his doubts until I had proven that
I could carry on in the "tradition." In other words, he gave me
time to show my mettle. Thank you, Jack.

Jack Smith's columns (five days a week) in the *Los Angeles
Times* have made him Mr. L.A. With permission from the paper,
he wrote longer, reflective pieces for us. As a reporter, he knew the
foibles and fables of our city life and described them with humor,
nostalgia, and irony.

We had no trouble getting on keel. He's a gentle man—even
humble. His pattern was to phone and tell me what he had in mind
for an article. If I agreed, and had no alternative suggestion, he
would write it and deliver the manuscript in person. We would
chat awhile and I always phoned him after I had read the piece. He
was grateful for the call. This was no false humility. He was a
newspaperman and wanted a word from the editor. He never took
off his professional hat. Sometimes he'd come in and say, "I really

JACK SMITH

don't know about this one. If you don't like it, don't use it." Or, "Do you really like it? Will it work for you?"

Only once did we have a problem. He was going to Russia on a vacation with his wife, Denise. I suggested—since she was the avid photographer—that they do a photojournalism impression together for our foreign travel section. They agreed. Denise took rolls of film, but when they returned to the States and developed them, most were blank or blurred—the fault of the mechanism or something. We could not let this trip go to waste.

We decided that Jack write a text and captions for the dark photos describing what the shadows probably were. He came by with the article, but I was out to lunch, so he left a note.

> Dear Frances: Here is the story and I think it's funny. That's all I'm going to say. If the pictures are unusable we have several that aren't quite as bad, and I can rewrite to suit. (Alterations free.)
>
> If you do go through with this, do you think you could use a credit line saying, "Photography by Jack and Denny Smith?"
>
> That would make me equally guilty whereas some readers may not think I have made that clear in the text.
>
> I will try to call you later today to see what you think about the art. Yours, Jack.

The article was hilarious and of course we gave Jack and Denny a shared credit. (Fortunately, Denny had and has her own successful career totally unrelated to photography.) Reader response was full of empathy and amusement. Many had suffered camera frustration themselves. At least Jack had suffered no loss of memory. His text proved that they were there and saw what the photos did not reveal.

Aside from this memo, Jack and I exchanged no other letters, but an inscribed copy of his book *The Big Orange,* a collection of essays about Los Angeles, speaks to our compatible working friendship: "For Frances, whose love is more important to me than her money. Jack Smith, June 30, 1976"

Much of the time, Jack Smith explored the city in his own way, but whenever I suggested a topic, he was willing to try it. An example is his article on the Korean population of Los Angeles, (May, 1976) which follows.

■

L.A. with a Korean Accent

BY JACK SMITH

In time, no doubt, the Korean culture will be adulterated by the hamburger, the taco and the pizza, but in this early period of the exodus it remains in a state of relative purity.

Anyone driving along Olympic Boulevard between Vermont and Western avenues is usually preoccupied with whether the green lights will turn red before he comes to the next intersection, or vice versa, which is perhaps one reason why so few of us have been aware of an astonishing new ethnic enclave known as Korea Town.

It is as if the entire population of a city the size of Santa Barbara, speaking and reading an alien language, had moved into the Los Angeles metropolis almost overnight and gone unnoticed except by their immediate neighbors.

It isn't that Korea Town is shy. For several blocks along its two main streets—Olympic and Eighth Street—it proclaims its presence with large, bright, fresh, commercial signs in Oriental characters which even to the English-reading eye seem somehow different from the more familiar Chinese and Japanese characters. The word Korea or Korean is also much in evidence, coupled with such commonplace neighborhood words, in English, as market, bakery and restaurant.

But only gradually does it grow on the motorist, merely passing through, that something is happening here besides just another outcropping of the city's Asian population, or another infiltration of a deteriorating middle-class stronghold by a migrant ethnic group on the climb.

There is a newness overall, not only in the inscrutable signs, but also in the goods seen through the market windows, in the faces of the pedestrians, in an air of optimism and vitality that is somehow reminiscent of street life in the days after World War II, when the veterans came home to settle in, raise families and make it.

In statistical terms, the explanation of this phenomenon is that Korea Town is the heart, the new capital, the city within a city, of 70,000 Koreans, most of whom have emigrated from their homeland to the United States within the last five years. In all, perhaps 200,000 have come to America from South Korea, but more have settled here than in any other city.

Unlike some other immigrant waves, the Koreans have not scattered into the homes of relatives and sponsors, nor found concealment in the multitude. Instead they have concentrated, planted their cultural flag, demonstrated a remarkable grasp of American-style private enterprise, and set out to work hard and live the good capitalist life.

Like enlightened conquerors they have occupied a declining neighborhood, one that was being gradually abandoned by its predominantly middle-class Jewish populace, leasing or buying office buildings, temples, storefronts, houses, apartments and vacant lots, and adapting them overnight to their own life-styles and enterprises.

In time, no doubt, the Korean culture will be adulterated by the hamburger, the taco and the pizza, but in this early period of the exodus it remains in a state of relative purity, as I learned when I ventured into one of the many Korean markets to be found in the neighborhood.

One need look no further than the doorway to see that the staple of the Korean diet is rice. Piles of it stand in twenty-five-pound sacks, like walls, at the front of the store. A second staple is evident in the large whole fishes, of a species I am not fisherman or gourmet enough to identify, stacked to the gunwales of cold boxes at the rear of the store.

Most of the shelves, not just some in an ethnic corner, are given over to exotic delicacies: salted oysters, codfish, baby clams, yellow corbina, anchovy, cuttlefish and shrimp; hot seasoned bean paste, dried persimmon, seasoned Korean cucumber, a bean mash made of onion, vegetable oil, potato, radish and mushrooms; long dried leaves of brown seaweed, dried laver, dried platycodon, dried eel, sliced hot peppers, golden curry, sesame seed and sesame oil, and gallon jars of kimchi, whose ingredients are Chinese cabbage, radishes, chili, garlic, onion and ginger root. Also, an abundance of Korean ginseng tea, which is not from a leaf but a root.

It was the immigrants' need for Korean food that gave Korea Town its initial reason for being. They had to live together near markets that would supply the ingredients, and markets were the first enterprises to appear. The new Americans also hungered for faith and credit, and soon they had their own churches and a bank.

I had a sense of the newness, vigor and optimism of Korea Town when I looked in at the offices of the Korean Association of Southern California in the Korean Community Center near Western and Olympic. This is a four-story building bought by the community with donations, half of the total coming from the Korean government through the local consul general.

A young woman in the outer office showed me into a private office where a man in a business suit stood on a chair, hanging a framed photograph of a woman. She hung at the center of a row of four men, all in the same-sized frames. On an adjoining wall hung a larger picture of Park Chung Hee, president of the Republic of Korea, in color.

Politely the man asked me to excuse him until the last picture was secure, then he stepped down. The persons in the five lesser pictures, he said in answer to my question, were leaders of the local community.

He asked if I would wait for the association's vice-president, a Mr. Kim, and asked the young woman to phone him. She got Mr. Kim on the line and Mr. Kim asked if I would wait until he could get there. It was the kind of politeness, of eagerness to make contact, to accommodate, that I encountered everywhere in Korea Town.

Meanwhile the man I had found hanging the pictures said he is Pyung Lee. He has been here from Korea only three years. His wife is Kwi Im Lee, a soprano of some prominence in Korea. She has begun to find an audience here, singing with the new Korean Philharmonic and at churches and in a recital at the Ebell Club.

I wondered if Pyung Lee was homesick. We had been looking out an east window of the office as we talked, straight across Korea town to the towers of the new Los Angeles skyline in the warm, clear, winter sky.

"I wish we had some snow," he said wistfully. "Seoul has four seasons. We can skate. But I like it here. The American life is busy."

Gene Kim, the vice-president, arrived in a small whirlwind of courtesy, enthusiasm and goodwill. Korea Town was happy to be discovered by the natives. It was hardly three years old, having been founded in 1973 by nine Korean merchants who wanted to draw the Korean immigrants into one community.

Kim was the first president of the association. One of their first ideas was a brilliant promotional stroke. They offered to put up signs, free, for any Korean business establishments that wanted them. That was in February 1973. They had soon erected sixty signs, and suddenly Korea Town existed. "Many Koreans saw the signs, and they came here."

Altogether in the metropolitan area, he said, there are already 70,000 Koreans though that figure is growing every day, with the arrival of each day's Korean Air Lines 747 from Seoul. At least 40,000 of them live in Korea Town, between Hoover, Crenshaw, Pico and Beverly; the others have gone to the suburbs or into Orange County, but they come to Korea Town at least once a week to shop, mostly for food.

Most of them have come to America since 1965, when United states immigration quotas were set up to 20,000. Thus 90 percent are first generation and obliged to deal with a language barrier and other aspects of cultural shock.

"To be Americanized they needed some help," Kim said. "There are many differences between Korea and American customs. In Korea there are not much automobiles. Here they have to drive.

The tax system is different. We had to make Korea Town, gather them here to get all kinds of information.

"We are teaching them to be Americans. They are isolated if they speak only Korean. That is no good. Public schools are important to teach the second generation, but it is most important to teach the first generation, their parents, or we will have a big gap between the generations. The kids can't understand their parents. We want them to be nice Americans."

Korea Town's look of affluence is all the more surprising since emigrating Koreans are allowed to take only $500 out of the country. Some doubtless have found devious ways around this restriction, but their money also comes from such old-fashioned American virtues as industry, thrift, dependability and enterprise. Though many are college educated and come here as physicians, dentists, pharmacists and engineers, their lack of English, and California licensing barriers, may force them temporarily into menial jobs. Husbands and wives both find work, and save. They borrow from banks to buy homes, or from the Small Business Administration to launch a business.

There are a thousand Korean-owned businesses in Korea Town already, offering everything from lessons in Taekwon-do, the national art of self-defense, to tax and money management counseling; from medicinal herbs to long-term loans. A directory of associations already organized in the new town shows an extraordinary compulsion toward community action. There are associations of artists, musicians, dentists, doctors, Christian youth, ministers, nurses, herb doctors, pharmacists, senior citizens, engineers and women, among others.

Korea Town was hardly a year old before it held its first festival and parade, not overlooking the American-style beauty pageant. It was so much fun that they did it again last year, and the third annual festival will be held this coming September.

Koreans also understand the nature and uses of political power, and are not unaware that in clinging together, in one neighborhood, they are more likely to be heard. "We can gather our opinions," said Kim, "to show what we want."

Kim thought that maybe half the Koreans in Los Angeles had

come originally from North Korea into South Korea as refugees. "Most are very friendly to America. Korea was thirty-six years under Japanese rule. In 1945 we got liberty. The American government tried to make a nice Korea. We know. The Communists wanted to make a Red Korea. They killed a lot of people. I was at that time in North Korea. I saw a lot of people arrested by the Communists. I am also a refugee from North Korea. Many North Koreans settled down in South Korea, but they were uneasy. If the North Koreans come down, they would be the ones arrested."

But there are also some in Korea Town who will tell you they are refugees from *South* Korea and the repressive policies of President Park. Some say they are spied on and harassed by agents of the South Korean government, and that the consul general's office tries to discourage criticism of Park's government.

This makes Kim sad. "It is a shame. There are just a few people in the anti-Korean government movement. They hurt Koreans too. We make money, we pay taxes, we live free. We don't like to be divided. We don't like to hurt our homeland, our mother country. We don't like to hurt ourselves. They [the government] don't bother us. They just have an interest in us."

At least 90 percent of the Koreans in Korea Town want to become naturalized, Kim thought. "We live in the U.S. We like to be American citizens. We like to see our second and third generations to be nice. You must be Americans, so you don't feel different."

Any vigorous young community grows its ostentatious successes. Hi Duk Kee, thirty-six, owner of the V.I.P. Palace restaurant and night-club, is a graduate engineer who knocked around Europe awhile before coming here seven years ago, virtually broke. His wife worked as a nurse and he worked at this and that until they saved enough to swing the purchase of a market on Olympic.

Two years ago, with his market doing well, Lee bought a corner on Olympic and built his palace, which indeed does resemble, in miniature, the pagoda-style Korean palaces in the picture books of Seoul. It is Korea Town's most exotic landmark.

The interior is ornately decorated, Korean style, with a ceiling of recessed red-lacquered panels, a water-wheel turning in a garden of plastic plants, Korean landscapes on the walls, a piano bar, and an American flag on a standard in the corner.

Lee's hostess, a lovely, slender young woman in a flowing gown with deep sleeves, stopped by our table to explain our Korean dishes and their preparation. The large seasoned radishes, for example.

"First we put in salt water. Yes? We drain. Wash. Put chopped garlic. Salt. Soya. Chopped greens. A little chopped ginger. Then we put in jar."

"It seems hotter than Chinese food," I said, chewing a bite.

"Oh! I forgot main thing. Chili powder!"

We had barbecued ribs, barbecued beef, broiled chicken and a small filet of fish, all on a sizzling platter; spinach seasoned with garlic, onion, sesame seed and sesame oil. It was similar to Chinese and Japanese food, but different, perhaps owing the difference mainly to chili and garlic.

The pianist had been playing Korean songs, but suddenly I became aware that he had segued into something familiar—"South of the Border." I wondered if the Korean words might say, "South of the Thirty-eighth Parallel," but dismissed the thought as a bad American joke.

After the plum wine Lee himself invited us into his tiny office at the rear of his nightclub to see the architect's rendering of the 100-room hotel he is building next door to his palace. It too will be pagoda-style, and Lee has no doubt about its future, with 50,000 Korean tourists coming to our shores every year.

The nightclub begins to swing at nine o'clock. A combo in scarlet blazers—saxophone, drums, piano—plays Korean songs, interspersed with American, and a beautiful young woman sings in her native language. (She was Korea's most popular singer, Lee discloses.) Guests leave their tables to dance.

But Lee's masterstroke of decor is a backlighted mural-sized color transparency of Seoul, the capital city, which glows above the bandstand like a view of the city at night through a window. A beautiful, modern city, from its skyline, and a sight that is sure to deepen the nostalgia of any Korean far from home.

A cross has been affixed to the arch over the doorway to the Young-Nak Presbyterian Church on Fairfax Avenue near Pico Boulevard, but in the great window underneath the arch the Star of David strikes an unexpectedly eclectic note.

The conversion of this handsome Jewish temple into a Korean Christian church dramatically symbolizes the metamorphosis of the neighborhood and the aggressiveness of the new immigrants. The Jewish congregation had been declining as the Jews began moving outward; the Korean population was expanding every day. Mostly Christians, since the missionary movements of the nineteenth century, the Koreans wanted churches, and couldn't wait to build. Among the immigrants were a hundred ministers, each eager to find his own church, gather his own congregation. Like the Young-Nak Presbyterian group, some raised the money to take over Jewish temples; some made do with houses or storefronts; one bought a Ralph's supermarket near Western and Beverly Boulevard and called it the Oriental Mission Church. Today the former Ralph's has a congregation of 500.

In the Young-Nak Presbyterian Church the seats are red-cushioned theater-style. The fine marble ark and pillars remain from the temple. The morning sun brightens the tablets of Moses, the menorah and other symbols of the Jewish faith in the stained glass windows. In the choir section sixty young Korean men and women, in maroon robes and gold collars, sing familiar Christian hymns in their native tongue. Their voices are sweet and disciplined, responding with exquisite harmony and modulation to their sensitive director. The pastor prays and gives his sermon in Korean, incomprehensible to American ears; but there is no mistaking the tone of earnest admonition and exhortation.

It was like an old oil painting, in which one scene has been painted over another, layer over layer: an Asian congregation communicating with a Protestant God in a Jewish temple.

After the services one of the elders, Chongnack (Nicholas) Chun, a real estate investment agent, told me how it had come about. The church had started out with thirty people. Now it had 600. For three years they had gathered in a rented building in Hollywood. Last September, with the help of the Korean Exchange Bank, they had bought the temple for $290,000, the Jewish congregation, which had moved to Culver City, carrying a second trust deed. To build such a church, Chun pointed out, would have cost one million dollars.

Sunday afternoons, after church services, the children of Korea Town begin arriving downtown at the First Methodist Church at Eighth and Hope streets, a vast old brick structure in which the Korean School has taken temporary quarters. Here the preschoolers—the precious cadre of Korea Town's second generation—begin their introduction to Korean language, customs and culture, and children of elementary and high school grades are kept intimate with the traditions they cannot find in their American public schools.

The classrooms are separated from one another by long dimly lighted corridors, but inside they are brightened by children's watercolors and their own eager faces and their exuberant reading from books that look very much like "Dick and Jane and Spot" in Korean.

In other rooms children are learning to play the piano or sing or dance, and in the gymnasium they are learning the moves and techniques of Taekwon-do, the karatelike art that dates from the Silla dynasty of 2,000 years ago.

Like everyone else in Korea Town, the directors of the school are looking upward. "We hope someday to have our own building," said Ki Saing Bai, chairman of the school board, who had come downtown to bring his own children. "We need our own playground. Our main function now is to raise financial support."

I wandered on down a corridor and encountered a small boy coming the other way. He looked about five. He might be lost, I thought for a moment, but he looked undaunted. In fact he looked rather jaunty. As we neared each other he gave me an interested, forthright examination.

"Hi," he said, in an accent as purely American as it is possible to give that fragmentary salutation.

"Hi," I said.

He was the second generation, coming on strong, and we had communicated.

M.F.K. Fisher

I FIRST MET M.F.K. Fisher through mutual Sonoma friends. She lived a short drive away in Glen Ellen, Jack London territory. Her all-in-one book-lined living-room-kitchen house was a still life in literature and food, and a reflection of her taste and style. She was taller than I imagined. Her gray-blond hair was tied back, leaving her face unadorned, direct, and as beautiful as her writing. She, alone, turned the "Art of Eating" into the art of living with her singular gift for combining both arts.

We discussed the possibility of a series of articles on California eating habits, or childhood memories of holiday foods. She was interested in the western focus. She had grown up in Southern California and thought it might be fun to reflect upon it.

But M.F.K. has to decide at her own pace, and when I left, I wasn't sure whether she would or would not. I dropped her a note. It was clear from her answer that she had given the project a lot of thought.

> Jan. 20, 1978:
> Dear Frances: Thank you for your thoughtful holiday message. Your note came yesterday when I was writing my list for you. I hope we can exchange many more.

I plan fairly short pieces, of perhaps 1500 words, and even thinking of putting two or three into one little grab-bag. We spoke in terms of your using perhaps six a year, bi-monthly or according to your needs and wishes. I want to do more than I'll list here, and of course can send you a longer number of suggestions. Here are a few of the more "Californian":

California cooks: Callahan, H.E. Brown, Elen Zelayeia, Idwal Jones, etc., some firmly reputable, some more legendary. I have known some of them. . . .

Chili: Cal/Mex, Tex/Mex, with a few recipes.

Enchiladas: to include tortillas . . . very personal (as this all is) probably with a couple of recipes.

The Wappo: California Indian foods tied in with other American Indian dishes . . . a few recipes, mostly about corn.

The Beachers: Eating on California beaches . . . now, then . . . kelp, surf-fish, etc . . . recipes.

Slow Stuff: Very Western "easy does it" . . . stews, breads, stocks . . . then and now.

This may give you some idea of what I want to do. There are many more topics that I feel strongly about. My approach will be personal: Survival Kits for car-bus-train-lane; Strangies, who eat avocados with kirsch or live on concentrated root beer extract; the delicate science of the Kitchen Library and how I have solved it; Wines and Why Not, mostly about what I call Icebox Jugs. I also plan to sound off about the Pasta Syndrome, in California, and about some of my most hated culinary words, like Yummy.

And so on. It sounds like a mishmash and it is. But I plan to go ahead anyway, and if some of it interests you, that will be nice. I'd like to know how you feel, of course, and then ask you to discuss dates and fees and all that with [my agent] . . .

As you can see, this writing will be candid and occasionally critical and opinionated. I intend to enjoy it. And perhaps you will too. . . .

All best,
Mary Frances

M.F.K. Fisher

When I finished reading the letter, I let out a *Yahoo*, but replied as if I were in control of my job:

> Dear Mary Frances: I like your suggestions. If you want a tentative schedule it might be nice to start with the California cooks for the June issue, which means I would need the copy by March 10.
>
> "The Beachers" might be a good summer story for August and from there on we could work on an alternate month basis.
>
> If this puts too much pressure on, we can start the series in August; the copy deadline would then be first week of May. Let me know what is comfortable for you. . . .

She replied, April, 1978:

> Here is the top copy of a thing I've written about "The Beachers". . . . I hope you like it, and that it's what you want. If not, just say so and I'll try again. . . .

I didn't say no and she tried again and again. Our correspondence continued:

> Here is the story! I hope it's all right. I feel very strongly about the current Mexican-American "question" in California, especially, and deliberately avoided it, by going back a bit. . . .

From me:

> Dear Mary Frances:
> The California Cook piece is "delicious" mush or no. Thanks—I'll place it in the June issue. . . .
>
> For the next piece, maybe you'd like to edge up into history—e.g. what did the homesteaders bring to our diet—the influence of a breed of settlers of your choice. Once again, it's wide open. . . .

Mary Frances was delightful to work with, but no pushover. If, by chance, there was a typo, she let you know. And if a staff member dared to tamper with her sentence structure, the reprimands came. For example:

Dear Frances:

Thank you for sending me the two copies of the June issue.

I am returning tear-sheets from one of them, to explain to you, very regretfully indeed, why I feel badly about the piece as it was published.

I thought we agreed long ago that I would see galleys before they went to press. I've always found this mutually wise, to avoid possible embarrassments.

I do not mind the change of title, nor the many shifts in punctuation that I assume are tailored to the magazine's "style."

There are, however, some bits of re-writing that make the piece much more the copy-editor's than mine. For instance, I am probably incapable of starting out "In days past . . . " as in col. 2. In col. 5 there is another non-Fisherian re-write. But the one that really chills me is in col. 6, after something of a lead-up with "Of course it is almost impossible . . . " etc. etc.: I would not and could not write the sentence printed as "The love of cooking and then eating outdoors, under the sky."

It is not a sentence.

Here I remind myself of once when Julia Child was asked what she thought about margarine, and she said icily, "The word has never crossed my lips."

But *Frances*! . . . I don't *write* that way. . . .

I assume you let me send things to you now and then because you like my style. But if some well-meaning copy-editor, no matter how skilled and experienced, is going to do my punctuation as well as syntax, why bother about going outside your staff?

I hate to be stuffy about this. As I'm sure you know, I have no illusions about writing Deathless Prose. But if anything I send you pleases you enough to publish it, I want it to be the way I wrote it, at least as my own *Prose*. (I know each magazine has its own style-sheet, and I almost always agree with it.)

I do hope this small whimper does not arrive at a bad moment, and I send my best anyway and as always . . . Mary Frances

I understood her concern and replied immediately. I don't have a copy of the letter but her answer speaks for itself:

13.vi.79

Dear Frances . . . thank you for your very understanding letter.

I agree fully with you about keeping a close look on syntax and general style and so on, even if you are fairly sure of the author's skills. I also know that you must cut, for space. And I understand about the time-element in getting galleys back and forth (although usually I insist upon a pre-publication look with magazines . . .).

The one thing I do not like is a re-write, without permission. I don't refer to the change of a word or two, but I do mean to protest about whole phrases and sentences that are not space-savers but are contributions (unsolicited) from well-meaning assistants. . . .

Enough of that, with my thanks for your patience.

Yes, you suggested my doing something about homesteading, and it seems to have turned into a thing about yeast, and the first settlers here with their own "starters," and the miners' bread, and so on. I don't know if this interests you at all, and it's all right if it doesn't, but I'll send it along on or near the July 1 deadline you mentioned. (I am having troubles about getting things typed, and may have to do it myself, which means that it will come with sincere apologies!)

The thing for October sounds amusing. I'd like to try for it. I wonder what deadline you plan. We kept a very low profile in Whittier for Hallowe'en. Both Grandmother and the Quaker community frowned on it as pagan. But I have some firm thoughts about that, as usual. . . .

It's been too hot up here. Things are more tolerable today. The weather-boys predict a very hot summer. I don't mind it, but the petunias do.

All best . . .

Mary Frances

We shared a taste for honesty and a regard for each other's ideas. When she came to Los Angeles to accept the Robert Kirsch Book

Award—a much overdue regional acknowledgment of her international reputation—we had a warm reunion. Since then, a letter or a phone call has kept us up on matters of health, and seasons' greetings continue to mark the years.

For the past half a dozen years or more there have been many collections and reprints of her works as generations of new readers became acquainted with her. Recently, I took down a copy of *Sister Age* from my shelf. It is described as a book about aging, living, and dying. But Fisher defies categories, whether she writes about eating or other of life's processes. She evokes an image in the subtlest way, and throughout the pages there will be sentences like " . . . the salty water had rolled down from my half-closed eyes like October rain with no sting to it but perhaps promising a good winter."

A food writer? Food for thought, for emotion, for the aesthete's palate. If we are what we eat, Mary Frances makes better fare of us all.

■

Open Hearth

BY M.F.K. FISHER

A 2,000-year-old recipe? Stir together Native American, Spanish, Mexican, European, Asian and African ingredients; what do ya' have? California cooking.

Californians are good outdoor cooks, and have been for more than 2,000 years. They are hospitable, and blessed with weather that invites friends to meet together in a courtyard and share food that has been sending out its own sensory invitation to enjoyment, and drink wine that has grown nearby.

It is a truism to say that the Indians were here before "we" were. Increasingly, and rightly enough, such a statement is heavy with political and cultural and even moral overtones. The fact remains that "they" wandered down thisaway a couple of millennia before the so-called white men appeared here and managed in a relative twinkling to wipe them out.

Spanish missionaries led by Father Junipero Serra corralled many of the Indian tribes into submission, after 1776, and the Mexicans helped turn them into agrarians instead of nomads. The first Californians learned how to plant and then eat vegetables like squash and beans and tomatoes that were probably good for them, but they forgot how to move out of the mission compounds, which was not good. They also learned how to grow the hot peppers that the Mexicans brought with them, and how to boil beef with herbs and spices, and it is easy to imagine that along with their resignation to mission life, their courtyards and compounds grew more redolent and welcoming.

By the beginning of the nineteenth century, as people from eastward infiltrated the Indian-Spanish-Mexican culture building itself on the west coast of the continent, what is now called California cooking was thriving. Both missions and haciendas opened their doors to the men and occasional women who had survived long, hard travels to reach such a fair land. The church was generous in its ordained days of celebration, and there were increasing numbers of important weddings between old, rich families and the newcomers, and the weather was mainly beneficent for a continuing calendar of fiestas.

Any such event, whether to honor a saint's day or the birth of a new heir to an impossibly large land grant from Spain via Mexico, called for days and even weeks of feasting. "Come on over," a purely western message, often involved traveling several hundred miles, mostly on horseback. And sending out that warm, casual invitation meant mammoth and continuing preparations: meat was slaughtered, fields of vegetables and herbs were grown and devoured and then quickly grown again in the accommodating climate, kegs of wine were rolled out, and the roofless enclosures of every community along the coast stayed fumey and bustling. The food, roasting in pits and simmering in great kettles like the ones used to render tallow by both priests and ranchers, was hearty, simple and endless, and the wine kegs never stopped flowing.

And the fires of California cooking never went out. They still smolder in millions of barbecue grills throughout the Western world, in Cannes and Copenhagan as well as in Hoboken and Pasadena. In California, for instance, which by now has an increasingly rich heritage of Oriental influences overlaying the basic Indian and then Hispanic and Yankee cultures, there are people who have built Chinese ovens back of their ranch houses, copied from the one Trader Vic Bergeron still uses in his first restaurant in Oakland. His oven was adapted from what he had learned in Tahiti, probably. Now people in Fresno, for example, and in Tahoe, roast and bake California game and fish and breads in the same way the Chinese taught the Polynesians to do . . . basically the same way the Digger Indians had always done.

By now, Californians of many ethnic backgrounds either buy or make tortillas, and eat them in countless guises. In days past to find good ingredients for an ethnic specialty one went to the cultural "pockets" where they might be found. I remember that when I was growing up, we got supplies for our occasional exotic tablesprees from around the Plaza in Los Angeles. Mexican on one side and Chinese around the corner. (We never ate Italian food, which was certainly available nearby, except for one stodgy Midwestern version of macaroni and cheese. This was probably because once in Genoa my mother had seen a sheet of pasta drying over the back of a dirty kitchen chair, in what she felt was a very unhygienic way. . . .)

Today, almost any grocery store or supermarket carries not only commendable-if-commercial tortillas, but their *masa harina* for making from scratch. Many decent sauces and suchlike are in cans. The freshly made items are better, of course, but sometimes, even in this golden land, their makings are hard to come by.

There is no doubt that a regional style has evolved from this slow amalgam of the cultures that have taken root on the West Coast. It is a mixture of racial hungers and a shared nonchalance, so that a patio-supper can by now be a fine mish-mash of Vietnamese, Indian and Jalisco-cum-Detroit, and emerge as a subtle, orderly way to eat "California style." It will send out whiffs of herbs and condiments and even meats and grains that the first people here were innocent of, but it will be cooked and eaten outdoors, as it would have been hundreds of years ago in these same places.

If I were a woman of the Wappo tribe, which lived in and around the Napa Valley for many centuries, until the whites and then cholera wiped them out in 1833, I would prepare a feast outdoors because there was no alternative. It might be to celebrate the marriage of a son, and in that case his wife could not eat with us. But such niceties of tribal protocol are not part of how I would go about my duties, and here is what my husband would offer to our tribe:

> Dried strips of salmon
> Grilled quail
> Acorn mush
> Fresh or dried blackberries

The salmon would have been cured in the sun, on long, sharp sticks. My husband would have walked many days to the sea, to bring it back to our valley. The quail would be roasted whole, so that the feathers would burn off and the entrails would fatten and scent the meat.

As for the acorn mush, here is the well-tested recipe:

> 1 part pounded leached acorn meal
> 1 part or more water

Mix and boil in finely woven basket with red-hot stones as needed, until done to desired thickness. Serve warm or cold, eaten from cupped hands.

In order to make and serve this basic dish, the acorns must be gathered (first catch your hare, then cook it!), shelled, dried well in the sun, and then pounded into a rough mash or flour. Since acorns are strong in tannic acid, the mash would then be leached, by placing it in a hollow in the river sand, lined with pine needles.

Many baskets of warmed water would then be poured into the sieve, to drain out until the taste was right. The mash would then be dried in the sun, on a flat rock.

If I were a Wappo woman in the Napa Valley, 1,200 or even 200 years ago, I would sometimes make acorn mush from my stored supply of the dried nuts, and then add other things to it, to please my family and my tribe. Thin strips of dried fish or smoked deer were good, put in at the beginning, while the series of hot stones kept it simmering. Sometimes, to please the children, I added dried berries and some honey toward the end. (For the acorn bread, I would add a bit of red clay to the dough of water and flour, to cut the tannic flavor and act as a kind of baking powder. . . .)

Of course it is almost impossible for us now to guess the tastes of such simplicity. The Franciscans brought their Spanish spices and garden seeds, and the Mexicans added theirs. Then the Yankees came, from various racial backgrounds, with their many habits of seasoning and cooking. And by now countless other influences shape what is, and probably always will be. California cooking, ever new . . . new herbs, new methods and always an inherent easiness.

Another thing, though, remains unchanging for us, through all the centuries: The love of cooking and then eating outdoors, under the sky. It is an ingrained and probably atavistic need, here in this part of the country. So come on over . . . for something on the grill, and perhaps acorn mush!

Cows in the Belfry

. . . voices in the attic, and Hallowe'en lost in the ghosts of childhood

It has been said by onlookers and participants of Hallowe'en that, at least here in the United States, it is a rural festival, a bucolic ritual, at best/least a small-town happening. I think this may be true.

In countries where All Saints' Day, November 1, is a serious celebration both in church and at table, Hallowe'en means simply the night-vigil for beloved and respected souls before sermons and graveyard visits, and then the Cakes and Ale.

In a country as widespread and as ethnically rich as ours, All Saints' Day is less obligatory as a religious ceremony; the somewhat pagan activities of restless youngsters were, at least until this twentieth century, an accepted part of village life. Reports of Hallowe'en "pranks" showed up in most of the so-called humorous writings until 1900 or so in this country, before Mark Twain and after, and were viewed, and even accepted, by their victims with Christian tolerance. It was the boys' "night out," the hallowed holiday for goblins and would-be ghouls.

I missed almost all of this backhouse brouhaha, because I was raised in Whittier, California, a small Quaker enclave when we moved into it in 1912. Members of the Friendly Persuasion did not hold with heathen behavior, any more than did our resident dowager, my sternly Campbellite grandmother. To any person who frowned, as did she, on Christmas trees as non-Christian trappings and frippery, a jack-o-lantern was almost obscene—although of course that loose word would not be used.

As I remember, on about October 20 a few grinning cutouts of orange pumpkins would be stuck to our schoolroom windows, when I was little, but our only contact with the realistic mischief of All Hallows' E'en was through my father. He had been born and raised in a village in raw Iowa country, where apparently the boys strong enough to survive their first fifteen years were as wild as ponies, and as malicious and inventive as poltergeists.

When Grandmother was away, and Father felt like telling us about what used to happen on Hallowe'en, his eyes would gleam and sparkle. Plainly, he loved to remember those free and freakish pranks. Mother at the end of the table would cluck and try not to enjoy herself, and we children, wrapped in our adopted Puritan behavior, would shiver with delight over our bread pudding.

The church belfry, Father said: that was the goal! A cow, a huge prize milkcow, must be hoisted up there, and from the inside of the church! It would kick and moo and bellow. The lady organist, braced for this annual disaster, would run whimpering across the village green. The mayor and the pastor would come, with the cow roaring and kicking, and people from all over would stand holding lanterns and peering up, and cheer the suddenly lovable young troublemakers, with forgiveness for their arduous and silly prank. (We never asked, as I recall, about how the frightened, hungry cow was brought down to earth again.)

Another Hallowe'en caper, in Midwest villages before 1900, was to tip over a few outhouses, especially when they were in use. Mother of course disapproved of this, but it seems that only mean cranky stingy people were thus persecuted by the local goblins, on the one night of the year when they had power.

All of this seemed exciting and strangely glamorous to children growing up in a more effete setting. Perhaps we knew that most of us would never have permission even once a year to be swept along by a demon energy, to tease and even to destroy. The best we could do would always end discreetly. . . .

The nearest we ever got to a pagan orgy was one Hallowe'en party Mrs. Thayer gave for several little girls on her ranch, safely outside the Whittier city limits. We all wore sheets, happily ignorant that in older cultures they were meant to be shrouds, with our young bodies dead in their wrappings. The ranch house was dark, and we were led through halls unfamiliar in the black, into cupboards and out, and the grown-up Thayer girls (then perhaps fourteen and sixteen) moaned and shrieked from the attic, or suddenly thrust out wet clammy hands from a broom cupboard as we shuffled toward the dimly lit parlor. It was *spooky!*

Once safely through the rites of initiation, we played Hallowe'en games. Apples hung on strings in a big doorway, and we had three chances to catch one of them with our teeth as they swung wildly around. We laughed cruelly when friends were even clumsier than we had been. There were word games too, all about dying and ghosts and other things not mentioned the rest of the year, and one of the Attic Voices came in as a hobbled old witch with a crooked stick, and told our fortunes, all of them doomful, in a dreadful cackle. Most of her teeth were blacked out with sticking plaster, but we knew that she was really Frances Thayer. Still, our hearts pounded.

Then we went out to the front porch, and bobbed our faces with increasing bravado into a big washtub for more apples floating in it. It was against the rules to bite into one of them if it touched the edge of the tub. It was against the rules to take a deep breath and go clear under and pin an apple to the bottom. It was messy frustration all 'round, and on looking back I don't see why some of us did not burst out crying and ask to go home—except that it was such fun to wear sheets over our school clothes and get wet and untidy, and we knew that Mrs. Thayer would finally give us the most delicious food in our worlds, because she always did.

By now I can remember only two things we ate that night: halves of hard-boiled eggs with monstrously evil faces painted on them in dabs of catsup, and orange ice shaped like little jack-o-lanterns, with chocolate eyes leering, and toothy wild mouths. There was an exotic fruit punch called the Witch's Brew, with hints of weird pulp and newts' tongues floating in it, made by our masked (Attic) servers, and then we were brought back to quasi-reality by countless cups of Mrs. Thayer's ineffably reassuring hot cocoa, and unlimited soft marshmallows to float and melt on it, and numberless sugar cookies cut into the shapes of witches on broomsticks, yowling cats, skulls with hollow eyes. We waddled out when parents came for us, our sheets dirty, our little bellies fat and happy. Up in the attic, there was one last mad scream.

Later, I am told, Hallowe'en took on some new restlessness in Whittier, and occasionally scions of the best families would be scolded by our police chief for soaping store windows and even tipping over trash cans.

Times were changing everywhere, of course, and not many years ago some more scions of the best families of another small town I was living in, far north of Whittier, went wild on October 31 and after a ritual tipple on a gravestone in the "pioneer" cemetery they knocked over one old marble marker. Then shame, guilt, fear turned into a mood of classic panic, and the horrified and exalted kids pulled almost every tombstone crooked or flat down before they fell sobbing into the hands of the local cops. Their families, after bailing them out on All Saints' Day, prevailed almost as gently as Quakers upon the town newspaper to forget the whole hysterical episode, and it boiled down to a mild editorial about the danger of Outside Influences upon our innocent young manhood, those hostages to fortune, and so on. Sturdy Native Sons of the Golden West pushed and pulled their forefathers' tombstones into place in the old burying ground, and most of the best families sent their scions away to good Christian schools as soon as possible.

A pagan influence had grown strongly, however, in the new century—a pack of lost souls needed to protest their exclusion from the elite of All Saints' Day. Small Hallowe'en sprees turned into potential brannigans and rumbles, at least out here on the Pacific Coast, and small-town cops from the Mexican border on up to Canada were ready, at the end of October, for anything from armed motorbikers in black leather to pipebombs from teenagers primed on pot and poteen. The goblin-uglies were trying to take over from the merely mischievous. . . .

Once in Hollywood when I was working there, I took my two little daughters out in Hallowe'en dusk for a prearranged trick-or-treat at a few neighbors' doors, and then we went to bed, after a ritual jelly bean apiece, and sometime after midnight our own doorbell rang and several voices below our streetside windows started yelling crudities and demanding that we let them in. "Trick or treat! And right now!" they bellowed, and hammered and pounded. I know I felt frightened, but I fooled them into thinking there were more people in the house than three little old ladies, and they did go away, still yelling and laughing, bent on scaring rather than harming their haphazard targets. Nobody in our neat upper-class neighborhood bothered to alert the police, nor did I.

Myself, I felt more depressed than frightened, not so much by the latent power of this pack of adult pranksters as by their using an ancient ritual of mischief-making, usually practiced by children, as a rough threat. They could never be hell's fallen angels, I prayed as I knew we were alone and safe again, but were only a sad remnant of earlier nights when there may have been no cow for them to hoist up into the church bell tower, not even an outhouse to overrun.

By now I am told, town councils arrange Hallowe'en festivities with psychological advisement: elementary schools march in costume parades; the high school kids have a barn dance, with fireproofed bales of hay set around the edges of the gym, and girls in long granny-aprons and painted-on freckles; junior service clubs and senior citizens hold their own carefully managed parties to keep us all from going heathen at least one night in the year, and tipping over a couple old tombstones and maybe dropping a mild cathartic in Aunt Mabel's tea. Mischief is sternly controlled. A whisper of disco music brightens the suburban fringes of what is left of the American Small Town, but at least it helps keep most of us potential poltergeists off the streets on October 31.

We do not bob for unsanitary apples any more. Instead we go with docility to our appointed schoolgrounds or country clubs, wearing Dracula masks and false noses. Innocence is perhaps comparative bliss in this pattern of our progress, and I feel glad that my father could boast happily of his country-bumpkin tricks. I am even glad that some kids in abandoned cemeteries have experienced one whiff of the god Pan's frightful magic, when willy-nilly they have capered wildly past all the graves, knowing for at least once in their lives that they were born free.

They all needed to be strong, to carry cows up narrow stairways, push over marble urns and obelisks, and so did a covey of little girls have to be brave socially and morally to go to Mrs. Thayer's secret orgy and survive through it all to her hot chocolate. As grown men called for whiskey, and adolescents found solace in beer and wine, so we smaller ghosts needed our own chaste stimulant, and here is about how Mrs. Thayer made it for us. It is a sure guarantee of serenity, after no matter what seasonal caperings at no matter what ages, but perhaps especially around Hallowe'en.

GOOD HOT CHOCOLATE
2 oz. (2 pieces) unsweetened chocolate
1/4 c. sugar
pinch salt (optional)
1 c. boiling water
3 c. hot scalded milk
2 dashes Angostura bitters *or* scant
teaspoon vanilla extract

Melt in double boiler over boiling water the chocolate, sugar and salt. Add water slowly, blending well. Then add hot milk, beating steadily with wire whisk or Dover beater. Let boil one minute, still beating, add aromatics, and, serve at once. Cover if not served, and beat again, removing "skin" first.

This of course can be made with two tablespoons cocoa to one ounce of chocolate, omitting sugar if the cocoa is sweetened. And grownups can use equal parts thick cream, strong coffee, and dark rum instead of the three cups of hot milk. This brew is for very strong *old* ghosts, any night of the year. Meanwhile, the secret is to beat things steadily and well. . . .

ROBERT NATHAN

ROBERT NATHAN

IF EVER A serious writer transported me to his realm of fictional fantasy, it was Robert Nathan. Reading *One More Spring, The Bishop's Wife, Road of Ages, A Portrait of Jenny,* I floated on his air of whimsy and surrealism.

Once again, from the vantage seat of an editor, I was able to pursue a writer I had long admired. Nathan was by now near eighty yeas of age, probably unknown to a generation of readers, though his name appeared on late-night reruns of films that drew their life from his novels. And—he was living in Los Angeles. I dropped him a note. His answer (October, 1975) was discouraging.

> You're very kind to ask me to write for *Westways,* because I enjoy reading it; but to tell you the truth, I am too old; I cannot think of anything to say about Los Angeles that would be of interest or concern to anyone, without digging into layers of enthusiasm and irritation (or even deeper) for which I no longer have the stomach nor the strength. But thank you for thinking of me.
> Cordially,
> Robert Nathan

I recognized the signs of depression in a writer who thinks he is no longer being read, but was not put off. I talked with John Weaver, a friend and contributor and also a friend of Nathan's. His advice was to keep after "Bob"; he would prod him as well.

I phoned Nathan from time to time, and one day he asked me to come by for tea. He lived in an Engish-style cottage above Sunset Boulevard with his English actress wife, Anna Lee. His long, lean face and dark, soulful eyes matched the tone of his letter. He was affable in greeting, but as we sat there sipping tea, he said he was disturbed by the hatred that causes so much violence in our time. He likened our times to the dark ages. Bands of men and women roamed the streets with intent to harm. Once they grabbed a purse and ran. Now they grab a purse, *shoot*, and run. He despaired, too, of the abuse of language by the young. He could not understand them. He did not want to write in anger—and he was angry.

Hadn't he always taken a course that veered him away from the unpleasant aspects of reality, I asked? He was younger then and could dream. It was hard to dream now when a nuclear future looked so bleak. He was also "growing out of health" and had less energy to create.

When we parted, I tried to extract a promise that he would think about writing. It took almost two years to draw him out. The piece he finally sent us in May, 1977 was a profile of his friend Leonard Wibberley, a vigorous Irishman and author of *The Mouse That Roared*, the most famous of his many works. Nathan was able to write about Wibberley because Leonard made him feel good. Leonard, whom I later met and who also became a contributor, was a bearded outsized leprechaun who could make the heart sing. Given an adequate amount of ale or Irish whiskey, he could also cry into said spirits and resonate a version of "Danny Boy" not easily forgotten. They were a good twosome sharing their depressions and their fantasies.

Later in the year, now that his pen had inked up, Nathan sent me a poem, "The Burro." I accepted it with a note:

> "The Burro" is beautiful and of course I can use it. Let's plan for December.

He replied,

> How grand that you are going to use my "Burro." It would be
> just right for December—the Christmas issue?

He then proceeded to suggest how it could be illustrated.

Over the next year or so, he sent other poems. It seemed easier
for him to write poetry than to trust his feelings to articles of
prose. We published another page of his poems. After some months
he wrote:

> No one has ever said anything, as far as I know, about the
> various poems of mine that you've published . . . so I feel rather
> hesitant about this. . . . Maybe you're being criticized, and peo-
> ple are saying what did you ever publish that stuff for anyway?
> . . . But if they aren't, would you be interested in another poem?
> I'm not quite sure of the title; I've called it "The Caged Bird,"
> but it really means the old, old poet no longer able to fly. Don't
> hesitate to say No, firmly.
> Fondly,
> R.

I knew about old poets, and young ones, too, who were fearful
of lifting their wings. I was touched and saddened, but glad that
we could open a door for him to fly through.

■

The Last Great Bard

BY ROBERT NATHAN

He is the most accomplished writer of our time. That is not to say
that he is the richest, the most famous, the widest read, the most
prolific—though he is prolific enough; I mean that his accomplish-
ments are the most diverse, and his skills astonishing. Each of his
books (and there have been more than a hundred in the past

twenty-five years) is, in its own way, a master work, whether a political satire, a book of travels, a view of history, a fantasy, an excursion into science-fiction, a detective story, a legend, a religious testament, a manual, or a poetic ballet. His voice, his speech—which is unique—is in all of them.

At sixty-two, he is a Patriarch. He lives with his wife, his youngest daughter, two younger sons, a daughter-in-law and a granddaughter, a dog and a cat, in a modest house in Hermosa Beach. It is a large family, almost a clan, for there are two older sons and an older daughter, attached but not domiciled. He is bearded, with the look of a sea captain, or a Gaelic chieftain; he is a Celt, and he is known as Himself.

His name is Leonard Wibberley.

He is, in fact, a Renaissance Man, set down in this twentieth century; a philosopher, a scholar, a theologian, a wit, a man of action, an historian—an expert on cannibalism—and a man as at home beneath the sea as on it. And like other great Celts before him, a founder of kingdoms—or at least a Grand Duchy; for didn't he found the Grand Duchy of Fenwick, that went to war with the United States, and won it?

A man, in short, to stand in awe of, or to rejoice in, depending on his mood. For he can thunder as loud as Conn of the Hundred Battles, or sing as sweetly as the bards of Aneurin and Llywarch, or argue as wisely as Merlin; he can whittle a fiddle from a piece of wood (he has made two fine violins and a cello from the finest grained spruce sent to him from Idaho). He has written books on violins, on scuba-diving, on sailboats and sardines.

He took me sailing once, years ago, on the ketch he had sailed twice to Hawaii in the Ocean Races; we travelled gently up and down the coast, in sight of the Marina, on a sea described to me as a millpond. I was seasick.

Yet whenever I see him, I am reminded of tall ships and great voyages, and the free blue air of ocean blows over me.

Here is his own account of another occasion: "It was a wonderful trip. Such larks, as Tiny Tim remarked. Jumping off the end of the boat with a rope tied around us, in mid-Pacific and being dragged through the water which was all azure and argent—

The Mouse that Roared

BY LEONARD WIBBERLEY

The army of the duchy of Grand Fenwick marches off to war with the United States. It's a perfect logical war; the duchy—all fifteen square miles of it—has figured it out: it will lose the war, of course, and then in due course it will be rehabilitated by the United States to the tune of several millions of dollars, thus avoiding bankruptcy. We see the army—all twenty of them—drawn up in review before the Grand Duchess . . . the sun glinting and gleaming on the great eagle banner, on the swords and helmets of the three men-at-arms, on the armor of the twenty archers, clothed, as the author tells us, *in mail shirts worn over leather jerkins and buff trunk hose, their six-foot bows slung across their backs, their buckles on their bare arms and their quivers bristling with arrows.*

There was the beat of a kettle drum and the blowing of a trumpet and the group followed Tully out of the courtyard down the hill and over the bridge to the border of the duchy. Little children lined the roads and applauded. Old men and young women marched alongside. They sang the ancient war song of Grand Fenwick, "The Crooked Stick And The Grey Goose Wing." Some cried and some cheered and all felt very brave.

Outside the border of the duchy the little army changed into civilian clothing and caught the bus to Marseilles.

catching dolphin on a lure made out of a teaspoon battered flat and with a hank of nylon cord at the head of it, climbing the foremast to reeve a halliard that came unstuck, and holding Bahai in the teeth of a 35-knot wind and yelling my head off in sheer delight.

"You should have been along, Bob, and hang seasickness. A week at sea, and you would have been in Paradise."

Or, of an earlier voyage: "I have been trying for days to fetch the Aran Islands in a pucan—a fishing smack—but the wind would not serve. Finally we went out for a sail and it was wonderful though Kevin was sick. There were big ocean rollers to contend with and a boisterous wind and the pucan drove into the seas and shuddered and tossed and flung about with them. I had the helm and the fisherman seeing the wind piping up more turned to me and shouted:

" 'Would you like a little more sail on her?'

" 'I would,' I said.

"So instead of reefing down, we broke out a staysail to everyone's delight (except Kevin, groaning in the bilge) and tore along with the determination and fury of the *20th-Century Ltd.* ploughing up the Grand Canyon. Never had so much fun in my life. There were a number of rocks about, some partially submerged with the seas breaking the most entrancing blue green over them. All these rocks have names—but names unlike any others I have heard. There was Cheeli and Cheelimor and Ogram and Leenane and so on—wild ancient names which without a doubt date from prehistory. The pucan handled wonderfully, very quick on her helm and yet she did not fight it too hard. When we got ashore, I learned that she was eighty years of age, which would not have comforted me out among the Atlantic rollers."

How Leonard managed to get the *20th-Century Ltd.* to the Grand Canyon, I do not know; but my heart goes out to Kevin.

Born in Ireland in 1915, Leonard spent his boyhood, from the age of eight, in a convent in England, and during the Great Depression made a precarious living playing the fiddle in the streets of London. How he got from the convent to a fiddle, I do not know, but the Lord must have loved him even then, for no matter how much his heart was in it, he is no great fiddler even today. *(But for all that, good enough to earn a seat in the New Loyola-Marymount Chamber Orchestra; and before that, among the second violins of the Redlands Symphony.)*

From then on, it was chancy going. There were years of newspapering: in Trinidad, where he edited the *Guardian,* and also the *Evening News,* and sailed his sloop among the islands; odd jobs, working in the oil fields; a marriage which ended badly. And then

Something to Read
BY LEONARD WIBBERLEY

There was no Time in my childhood nor in yours if you were ever really a child. Day followed lovely day through summer, autumn, winter and spring. No end was ever in sight, nor any change beyond that of the seasons ever dreamed of. Adults, living in another dimension, ruled me with concepts which for me were dreamlike and unreal. My face must be washed, my hair must be combed, I must get up at such and such a time and go to bed at such and such a time. . . .

Poor adults. I was pure spirit and they had to make a mortal out of me, and that is the sad task of all adults who themselves were once pure spirit and who have, for the time being, lost that only true kind of existence, substituting for it one that is necessary for the body and bewildering to the soul.

to Canada, in search of bread or glory or the wild goose . . . from there to a naval shipyard at Rhode Island, and from there in turn to New York and the Associated Press. Back to England—and to New York again, this time as Foreign Correspondent. But he was unhappy and cold, his wife had left him, and he asked a travel agent to send him somewhere warm; and so he came, finally, to California.

He found himself (under God's hand, although he didn't know it) in Turlock, whose newspaper needed an editor; and there, too, he met Hazel, part Indian and part goddess, a teacher in the local school, and married her. But first he had to go to Reno to get a divorce from the other one; and in Reno he did what he could to make some money, for he had all too little. He laid rails for the railroad, and did other odd jobs, until the time was up, and he could marry again. His friend Bill Dredge got him a job on the *San Rafael Independent* for a while, and Hazel gave up her teaching; but it was too small a job in the end, particularly for a Foreign Correspondent, and he and Hazel moved on south, to Los Angeles, where he found work—of a sort—on the *Los Angeles Times*. It led, finally, to the copy desk, but not for long: meanwhile he had written a juvenile, *The King's Beard,* and after a year of hassle and rejection, he found a good agent for it in New York, who got it published, and one or two other juveniles besides. But they were child's play. In 1954 he wrote his first novel, *Mrs. Searwood's Secret Weapon,* and left off newspapering; and in 1955 *The Mouse That Roared.*

He was launched, there was a new novelist in the world. He bought a tiny house in Hermosa Beach, a house with four rooms no bigger than a sigh—and one of them a bathroom—and one of them a midget study which he shared with his three children, Kevin, Tricia and Christopher; they slept in it at night when he was finished writing. For the rest, there was Hazel, pregnant; and a great white English bulldog named Tully. In time the fourth child, Arabella, was born, and they moved to a slightly larger house in Manhattan Beach, from which, two years later, he piled them all, Kevin, Tricia, Christopher, Arabella and Hazel (who was pregnant again) and Tully, and the luggage, into a small English Rover, and set off for Portugal, due mainly, I think, to a desire for sardines. It had come to him one day on a mountain-climbing expedition; he had brought along a can of sardines for his lunch, and when at last, weary and hungry, he sat down to eat, he discovered that he had forgotten to bring a can opener. And as everyone knows, there is no way to open a can of sardines without a can opener; not even a rock will do it, or a penknife.

Out of such frustrations, whole love affairs have been known to develop. In any case, out of that one, came one of his most delightful travel books, *No Garlic in the Soup.* And in Portugal, Rory was born. Cormac came later.

It was in 1960, or thereabouts, that he joined the IRAIRAOV, a literary group of insufficiently recognized and inadequately recompensed authors of outstanding volumes. Its members consisted of its president, John Weaver, the biographer of Earl Warren, and, more recently, researcher and author of *The Brownsville Raid;* Turnley Walker, author of *Rise Up And Walk;* Robert Carson, author of *The Magic Lantern;* and myself, author of *The Bishop's Wife.* To be president, one must have gone through a more discouraging time than anyone else, or have suffered a more spectacular disaster. The presidential campaigns were fiercely waged:

TO: All Hands
FROM: Your Beloved President-elect (maybe)
SUBJECT: Confounded Chicanery, by God

As you know, at the last meeting of our organization, the Carson-Wibberley axis in a brilliant maneuver which will be studied by parliamentarians for many years to come, managed to unseat our beloved President John Weaver (known in San Francisco as the Diamond Jim Brady of the Hungry i).

There then followed an even more brilliant parliamentary maneuver. Choosing a moment when Carson was deeply engaged in conversation with the Goddess, Weaver was discussing the symptoms of caviar poisoning, Nathan was denouncing Knopf, and the members of the auxiliary were discussing babies, I proposed myself as your beloved President. The question was put to the house and those supporting my candidacy asked to vote "Aye." I did so. I then asked in a quiet voice whether there were any contrary minded.

Carson was still deeply engaged with the Goddess.

Weaver was discussing caviar poisoning.

Nathan was denouncing Knopf.

There being therefore no opposition, my election was carried without dissent, and I was overwhelmed with congratulations by my friends—meaning me.

Since then, however, some absentee ballots have been coming in.

I naturally suspected that these were bogus since none of them favored my candidacy. My suspicions were however fully confirmed when I received one particular ballot attributed to myself and casting my vote for Weaver. It was written on Hungry I stationery.

What I want to know is—am I your beloved President, you stinkers, or am I not?

I rise from sickbed, where I have been detained these several days with gout, to put this question to you. Do you believe in that democratic process whereby I won the election fair and square? Or do you want to throw the whole thing open again to the membership so you can rig it for yourselves?

> Yours in pain and wrath,
> Leonard Wibberley
> Beloved President-elect (maybe)
> Inadequately Recompensed and
> Insufficiently Appreciated Authors of
> Outstanding Volumes Inc.

After all, honors do not come easily to a writer—particularly to one whose home is west of the Wabash. To the Eastern Establishment, California is far away, and altogether strange; a New Yorker, a Bostonian, a Philadelphian thinks of California the way a Londoner thinks of Australia. Yet Leonard Wibberley's work has a broader reach than any writer I know of, east or west—from the hilarious political fantasies of the "Mouse" series, that history of the Duchy of Grand Fenwick (somewhere between Luxembourg and Liechtenstein)—to the mystic beauty of his *Meeting With A Great Beast*; from the joyous *Encounter Near Venus* (later made into a ballet), to the scholarly and deeply felt Biblical novels, *The Centurion*, and *The Testament of Theophilus*; from the delicious travel books, the voyages to Ireland, Portugal, the South Seas, to the classic simplicity of *The Hands Of Cormac Joyce*; from *Quest of Excalibur*, to a long poem about a cat; from Father Bredder, the detective-priest, to a vice-president eaten by cannibals. To say nothing of the lives of the early Presidents and the great Pirates . . . for children, of course.

And all in Leonard's great flowing style, full of laughter and delight, beauty, wonder, and indignation.

I knew him first a long, long time ago. We met—or at least I saw him—during the last high-gathering of the Celts on the shores of what is now the Caspian, where the great river—the Volga—comes down to meet the sea. That is where we separated, the main part of the tribe pushing on westward among the Scythians to the great ocean, to Brittany and the damp islands beyond, to Cornwall and Ireland: while others—my own family among them—turned

---

Quest of Excalibur

BY LEONARD WIBBERLEY

The King's hair hung down to his shoulders and was raven black, as was the hair of the early Celts before their blood was mingled with that of the fair-haired Saxons and Jutes and Angles. His beard was black too, a full black mane that came down to his chest and gave him an authority and majesty as strong as a lion. He wore a cape which was fastened by a cord of golden cloth around his shoulders and under this, a tunic of doeskin. The cloak was dark, but little globules of mist clung to it, scintillating little spheres which caught the light of stars and turned it into a white fire. Arthur then was outlined in a cold, pure light. Across the King's shoulders hung a baldric and from it, the top just visible under the cloak, was hung a big jeweled scabbard.

---

south, crossed the snowy mountains—passing the remains of Noah's Ark on the way—and in the highlands of Mesopotamia, by the headwaters of the Euphrates, founded Ebla, whose most illustrious king was named Ebrum. It was from Ebla, many centuries later, that Abraham went forth into Ur of the Chaldees.

It was all thousands of years ago. Deny it if you will: but the last of the old Celtic Bards lives today in Hermosa Beach, plays on an Irish harp, and writes books about elephants and leprechauns and my own very, very distant relatives in Jerusalem.

■

The Burro

BY ROBERT NATHAN

We traveled across the desert together,
My burro and I:
Across the brown desert,
Leaving behind us the loud voices,
The city, the dismay and confusion.
And I said to my burro,
'Small friend, patient, obstinate beast,
Where did you come from?
Do you have memories of another land,
Another time?'
And my burro said to me,
'I remember.
I remember a desert, rockier than this,
And a man and a woman and a child
Fleeing from the king's soldiers.
And once I came into a great city
White and shining in the sun,
And there was a great sound of voices,
And the waving of many branches,
Branches of palm.
And someone rode upon my back
Among the multitudes—
A man.
I do not know who He was.'

The Caged Bird

BY ROBERT NATHAN

Morning again. And in the summering elms
The flit of wings among the harboring leaves,
Into the shadows and then out again.
Above, the sky is open as the sea.
There is a world of wonder to engage,
Sounds, sights and visits in the shining air,
The windsong hum of bees,
Colors, and the excited talk of birds—
A day's full business in and out of trees,
And nests to build, and orisons to make.

But in this sunless clime
The day is long no matter when I wake;
For here, behind the withes of my cage
I see no grasses bending in the breeze.

I can remember from another time
How free it felt, so joyously to take
The morning light, and from the shadows climb
To the clear ocean of the sunlit air—

No more, no more—
Who now with unavailing wings must nurse
All he can see from out his cage's floor:
One silent corner of the universe.

WILLIAM SAROYAN

WILLIAM SAROYAN

H OW DID IT begin with Saroyan? One of our contributors, William Childress, a highly-charged freelancer who
lived in Fresno profiled the voluble Armenian, who thirty-odd
years back refused to accept the Pulitzer Prize for his play *The
Time of Your Life.* The reason? Not because he didn't think he
deserved it, but because he thought they should have given him the
prize for his earlier play *My Heart's In The Highlands.* Saroyan's
arrogance had softened with aging, and the Childress article captured the change. It then struck me that it would be a lively
thought to have a current piece of writing by Saroyan to run in
tandem with the profile. I wrote him. He answered immediately on
"Sunday, September 9, 1973 at 2 P.M."

> Dear Mrs. Ring: Having your very nice letter permits me to
> tell you how much I think of *Westways.* . . . And because you
> have been kind enough to invite me to send something here is
> The Celebrated Jumping State of California, or The Song of
> California—the sub-title can be deleted, and probably should be,
> but having only a moment ago added it, I must have believed it
> was useful, so I am letting it stand. As you will notice I have very

carefully improved the story in handwriting, and I hope there will not be too much work in making out my calligraphy, if that's the word. If you like the piece, I'll be quite pleased. If you don't, I will go right on liking *Westways,* and will very likely send in another piece (although I am getting ready to return to my home in old Paris) (actually the first area of the city, just back of the Opera). Is it permissible to spoof California? Well, I think it is not only permissible it is necessary for all of us to spoof everything, including God, because as soon as we are either unable to do so, or afraid to do so—for whatever reason—we may know that there is no love left in us, and that there can't be very much life left in us, either!

In 1960 in Moscow, I told one of the bigshots of Culture that Russia was making a terrible mistake in not embracing Pasternak and his novels and his poems, but the poor man said No, no, he is our enemy. And I said, But you can only grow in your enemies, and surely you must not believe that Russia is so fragile that anybody at all can really damage it. And of course Pasternak loves Russia so deeply he is terrified of being banished to another country.—And now it's Solzenitsyn and the scientist whose name Sarkanov I can't even spell . . . most of them repudiating officially what we know they believe in. . . . Suicide by love and procreation? Is that what the mystical ecological tides in the soul of the human race is carrying us to? Again thanks, and I ran a line through the sub-title: it won't do, that's all. . . . Yours truly: William Saroyan

I was fascinated by the letter, which ran on from light to serious commentary on our societal dilemma, and was amused by the article which was a "spoof." It was written single-spaced on legal-sized onionskin paper, with not a breath of margin top to bottom or side to side. In this way he may have thought he precluded editing, especially as he had already scrawled his own ink notations here and there on the page. But we found ways to circumvent and paragraph the manuscript as well as to retype it. We had heard so many tales about his temperament and complaints about editors that we returned the corrected manuscript for his approval. I also phoned him to tell him that the manuscript was coming. He replied,

> Friday October 5, 1973, 1 P.M.
>
> Thanks very much for chatting with me on the phone and for sending the original ms with blue pencil work—it seems just fine. . . . Just for fun, here is a "painting" called Insects, which thrive in the front and back yards here. Thanks again, and all best. (Insects is painted on tissue paper from a book shipment because insects are so magnificently insubstantial—it seemed appropriate.) William Saroyan

The "painting," was a squiggly drawing not only on tissue, but folded into a letter-size envelope and signed: "William Saroyan, Thurs. April 26, 1973 9 P.M. #1 Insects." To this day, it hangs framed on my wall, paper creases and all.

This was a good beginning. Through the years, he continued to send in personal essays—not all of equal quality but all with the Saroyan touch—a charming turn of phrase or an off-the-wall subject in a style that bore his mark. What else could be expected from a man who lived in two houses, side by side in Fresno—one for working and sleeping and one for guests? When he needed a change, he went to his apartment in Paris for several months.

He sent notes now and then. On February 5, 1979, 4 P.M. he wrote:

> Dear Friend Frances Ring: . . . Here is "Visitors From Inner Space," which I hope you like, and will take pains not to lose the manuscript which is the only one there is, and return it to me after it has served its purpose. . . . I don't seem to be getting *Westways* in the mail (again). And I am not unaware that every time I write you I mention this or something like it. . . . How did the Anniversary go? Has that special issue come out? [We published a 70th Birthday issue.] I believe you know how much I admire the magazine—it is full of good stuff. . . . If this piece is no good please rush it back so I can send it to *The Nation* or *The New Republic,* and I'll see about fishing out something else and sending it along—but this does seem especially right for *West-*

ways, I think. . . . And tell me your own news—what all is going on, as they say. William Saroyan

I bought his submission and sent him a copy of the magazine. At the end of the year, I received a card from him:

December 25, 1979.
Dear Frances Ring
Happy grand 1980—but once again *everything* mentioned in your October 31st letter HAS NOT happened. No 1979 complimentary back issues. No Saul Bernstein Art work. [He had requested the art that illustrated one of his articles. The artist was flattered and willingly donated it.] Please look into this, for I do WANT *Westways*. All best, always, and thanks very much. Bill Saroyan. P.S. Please write.

I replied:

Dear Bill Saroyan: Thank you for your "grand 1980" greetings. I hope it holds wonderful new pleasures for you, too. Like a piece of art from *Westways* which is being mailed out today, certified, first class. Please let me know as soon as you get it.

Concerning the magazine, we have mailed out a year's supply to you. I think someone at the Fresno post office is enjoying them. I will try it once again. This time we will send it in two packets in the hope that at least one of them will get to you.

Again, thank you for your interest in *Westways*. One of my pleasures in the 70s has been to make your acquaintance through the mails, untrustworthy as they are. Very best.

We never met. But through his letters and writings he is personified to me. I hope his heart is at peace in the highlands.

■

The Celebrated
Jumping State of California

BY WILLIAM SAROYAN

I had no idea it was so complicated—getting license plates for an automobile bought in Europe and after four years brought to California, which, as the song says, is the greatest state of all. Which it *is*. But isn't it just a little overloaded with government?

Again alas it is. But if I may, perhaps I can put it this way: more power to you, California. Instruct your workers to keep the rules and regulations, and all will be well, most likely, except for one thing—the rest of the people will go mad. The poor people and the rich people, they will all go stark raving mad. But that will be just fine too, because there are governmental places for such people to be sent to, all fully staffed by government workers who are frequently slightly less mad, although supremely maddening.

California is heaven, as everybody knows. Willy-nilly, by hook and by crook, by geography and by climate, California has *always* been heaven, and I was born there. I grew up there, and watched California grow up there, too—from a small, unassuming heaven into a great, highly governed heaven, full of precious freedoms of all kinds, provided you fill out the forms, stand in line until you come face to face with the lady who has been learning with each new arrival, each new form, the way to get the form processed, and the new arrival put in his place—right smack in the heart of the asylum, in the secluded rural regions of San Francisco.

I wish Mark Twain were in San Francisco now, and I wish he had a car of some kind, and I wish he wanted to get license plates for it, because I believe that trying to get them would cut him to the quick—for a moment, at any rate—or cut him dead, or drive him straight to the loony bin, or even to Missouri, or headlong into New York—and from there straight on to London.

It might also drive him to the writing of an account of the awful—but in its way beautiful—experience.

Old Mark Twain wouldn't write like this. He was a young fellow when he was in California getting ready to write "The Celebrated Jumping Frog of Calaveras County," and he would really write. He was a kid in his early twenties. A hundred years later here I am in California, in San Francisco, in my late fifties, standing in line with a form filled out to the best of my ability, six or seven other documents filled out that over the months I have been advised by the Department of Motor Vehicles to get. I don't understand any of the forms, or the questions asked and answered in them. Documents are not my line.

My line is song writing. I'm a songwriter. I have always loved the song about California, and I have always wanted to write a new one like that, but I have never hit on how to do it so that the song would do justice to the place. But while I have waited, I have written short stories, novels and plays about California, and the grandeur and wonder of it.

If Mark Twain had stood in Line Number 28 as I had—there had been only five other California automobilists in Line Number 28, whereas in each of the eleven other lines there had been sixteen or seventeen automobilists—he wouldn't have failed to understand something about California that I *am* failing to understand. He would have had a grand time, and he would have written a grand story about it, and then he would have died of old age.

With all of my years of adult experience, added to which is all of my boyhood and young manhood experience, I might have been expected to have had a grand time, too, but songwriters learn slowly, they are the slowest learners of all, they are slower than any other category of human creative effort, most likely from being so everlastingly preoccupied with one great song each of them wants to write. But I *didn't* have a grand time. Just before nearly dying of confusion I went a little berserk as a matter of fact, and that's bad.

Waiting your turn in line in California, you must not go berserk, because it is a sure sign of a rotten character.

The first man in Line Number 28 is a Chinese of forty-five or so, who can't understand a word the lady is saying, but she goes right on making notes on various new forms she has brought forth, to suit his particular confusion, and as she makes these notes, getting her rules straight from various pamphlets and brochures, she says, "You've made an overpayment of twenty-two dollars. I don't know why you made an overpayment of twenty-two dollars. Where did you make the overpayment of twenty-two dollars?" After thirty-five minutes, and after calling over two other ladies, all the forms were piled up, stamped, clipped together, handed to the man, and he was told to take them home and get the original owner of the car to clarify the matter of the overpayment of twenty-two dollars. The man didn't go home, however, he only moved just a little to the right, so that the next automobilist might give the thing a try, and he stayed there. He just *stayed* there. Then two other experts came over to the Chinese and took the papers from his hand and went over everything again and came to the conclusion that he could be permitted to have his papers stamped as being in order, and the hell with the overpayment of twenty-two dollars, or the hell with human life, what good is it really when nobody's papers are properly filled out and hardly anybody knows why he has made an overpayment of twenty-two dollars?

Next in line was an old Italian who understood English, clearly spoken, but the lady looking after the people in Line 28 wasn't speaking clearly, although it was very probably English, certainly not Italian, and the impression he got was that he was in a lot more trouble than the Chinese had been in, so he asked several times, "What?" The lady told him what, but each time after she had finished telling him, he again said, "What?"

He was astonished. Some people are frequently astonished. And of course in the meantime the lady got out new forms and began jotting down numbers, names and words, talking steadily, which impelled the Italian to look around at the people waiting behind him, both asking for sympathy *from* them and expressing sympathy *for* them.

Again the experts were called in, again conferences were held, and again the papers were finally stamped as being in order, and the Italian, by now a little unhappy about ever having left Sicily, went away.

Next in line was a boy of eighteen or nineteen, but there isn't much point in giving an account of the rigmarole he was put through. The important thing is that in the end his papers were stamped OK, too, and he took off.

And so it was with the young wife whose baby was along, behaving beautifully, but again it was the same old story, although in the end it turned out happily, too.

And then it was my turn, and it *didn't* turn out happily.

I had filled out everything all wrong, the lady said, and this impelled her to ask questions which as far as I was able to make out were meaningless, so I was compelled to say, "I really don't understand anything you're saying. I was told to bring the car here for an inspection, and I've done that, and then I was told to go to any window from 18 to 28, and almost two hours ago I came here, to the line moving to window 28, because there were only four people ahead of me. I'd like to have my license plates."

The lady didn't like my language, and I don't blame her. In a way. I was near flipped, and she had surely already had a long, hard day—my sympathies go out to all government employees, of course, but that really doesn't help. It certainly doesn't help in the matter of hoping some day finally to write the great song of California. "Clerks of California, I sympathize with you" isn't a very good first line for a song.

The lady gave me a long patient look and then said, "I'm giving your form *this* stamp." She then stamped something mysterious on the form I had filled out, and on the forms she had brought forth, and then she said, "Now, how long have you been in business in California?"

Well, I just didn't know how to answer that one. There are questions that can't be answered, especially under certain circumstances, and this was such a question and such a circumstance. And there are certain askers of certain kinds of questions to whom it is impossible to make a reply, perhaps for the reason that the question isn't really clear, isn't really a question, and the asker is only talking out of an old established habit of making confusion.

At last, though, I decided I had better at least try for something.

"In business, in California?" I said. "I don't believe I have ever been in any business in California. Where does it say on that form that I am in business here?"

"You will have to answer all questions truthfully," the lady said.

Well, truth is something I have been concerned about all my life, but in this particular context there appeared to be a good chance that all of my concern might be instantly thrown out the window into the alley. "What questions?"

"Answer *all* of the questions truthfully, please," the lady said.

"I think I'd better have a chat with the manager," I said.

A guard told me to go to window 13, and there, after some time, the manager arrived, studied my name, my face, my documents, and then said, "I wish I could write half as good as you do."

"You must try harder," I said.

He opened a pamphlet and read something out loud, and waited for my comment. I said that what he had read had no meaning, and then he asked me to kindly wait a moment while he consulted somebody else. I waited fifteen minutes, and then he read the same thing again, but perhaps with more feeling. I decided I'd better not make any comment this time.

"Your writing has given me great pleasure," the manager said. I really wanted to be glad about this, and to be grateful to him for telling me, but I had used up the better part of the afternoon in failing to achieve something I had imagined was routine and would require surely no more than fifteen minutes.

I behaved very badly, and I'm glad I did. I picked up all of the papers. "I'm not sure I wouldn't rather leave California," I said. "I'm not sure I want the car any more."

"I only wish I knew how to write the way you do," the manager said.

"Is that so," I said. "Well, there's nothing to it, really. Just avoid going mad, being neutralized by the government, and I think everything will be all right."

And that was that, as the saying is. I drove to the public library, found a parking place, put a nickel down a slot on a meter, and then read that from 4 P.M. to 6 P.M. any car found in that space would be towed away. I had had my car towed away last year, and it had been a lot of trouble and expense getting the car back. I backed out of the space and looked for another place, but there wasn't any.

Finally, I drove to a place on Divisadero Street, where, for $1.99, I had the car washed. I was awfully confused.

How would Mark Twain have used this kind of material for a story? Would he have been able to get something celebrated out of it? Not a jumping frog, perhaps, but a little something or other? Because there *is* something jumping, and not just in Calaveras County, something's jumping in every county of the state. Is it the government? Or is it the people? Or is it inevitable?

I don't know. I'm a songwriter. I'm not very bright, but worst of all, most painful of all, I'm not very nice. I wasn't nice to the lady of Line 28, but now, at last, I'm sorry about it. "Lady, I really behaved very badly, and I'm sorry." And even though I tried very hard, I wasn't very nice to the manager, either. "Sir, I was entirely out of order when I saw you. I guess I wasn't myself. I really meant to be a good Californian, but I wasn't, and I'm sorry. I was paranoid, and I think you know what that means. It means I felt California was persecuting me, and that's very bad. California doesn't persecute anybody."

I had been wrong, smoking one cigarette after another, and not for an instant appreciating the privilege it is for me even to *be* in California again, in San Francisco again, partly alive, partly all right.

California, I ask you to forgive me. I know California is heaven, and if heaven's not my home, O Lord, where shall I go?

And how shall I write the great song of California?

Visitors From Innerspace

BY WILLIAM SAROYAN

A fairly wide variety of people of the world and especially of America have reported to the proper authorities sightings of unaccountable forms of fire, force and movement, as well as actual experiences with visitors from outer space, as it is called.

Carl Sagan, who teaches at Ithaca, New York, has pointed out on Johnny Carson's late-night talk show that it really isn't scientific to think of these optical and protean experiences excepting as very real examples of aberrational disturbances within the witness and not in the real world. Or words, or ideas, to that effect, at least insofar as I have been able to hear and interpret the words at that hour of the California night.

Well, what about visitors from outer space? I can't say, because I have had no actual experience with any such visitors, but Sherwood Anderson forty-four years ago at the height of his fame pointed out that he was frequently visited by unpublished writers who didn't want anything from him, they only wanted to see him, and to talk for a few hours, that's all, about life.

They came from everywhere to his door somewhere in Ohio, and Sherwood Anderson complained in a piece he published in the famous magazine called *Vanity Fair,* "But they don't bring anything."

Well, now, that is a valid complaint, most likely. Of course each of the visitors brings himself, but Sherwood Anderson clearly did not consider themselves one by one any order of gift, and what he clearly wanted from each of them was a gift, even if only a token one, such as a 1901 penny, a red pebble, a leaf from a eucalyptus tree, a small black kitten or a cork from a champagne bottle.

These visitors were quite simply the original visitors from outer space, and from Detroit, Cincinnati, Modesto or Seattle, although each of them looked (at least for the most part) as if they had traveled several million light years to get to Sherwood Anderson's door and to cry out with vigor and human warmth, "Hi."

Well, of course it may be that they had lately read Sherwood Anderson's story *I Am a Fool,* but at the same time had read around in Walt Whitman's *Leaves of Grass,* and had come to believe that after the instructions about civil disobedience put forward by David Thoreau—David? Really? It doesn't seem quite right, but that's the only name that comes into the writer's head, perhaps because of the other David and what he did to Goliath, as this David hoped to do to the local government about the local tax, or something.

After the instructions about eccentricity of lifestyle at Walden Pond—some say it was a puddle—and how to write clearly about grass and the little things that move in grass, just as neatly made and just as live as any human being—after *those* instructions, there were the very loud and joyous instructions from Walt Whitman to go forth in the world and to knock softly at doors, and upon having the door opened to cry out hi, as if saying, "I am your brother, we are kindred souls, many are the hours I have spent in a daze, puzzling over the structure of the common dandelion, many are the years I have wandered over the face of the earth seeking the answer to the basic questions, and so now here I am at your door, hi again, oh famous Sherwood Anderson."

Well, of course if Sherwood Anderson hadn't felt he had an obligation to these people, if he had been a more light-hearted soul, like Robert Benchley, for instance, he would have replied, "Would you please go say hi to Herbert Hoover in Washington? He's your man, he's the President, I'm only a humble poker-player and evasive writer."

But no, Sherwood Anderson had to make the fatal mistake of permitting the silly situation to become sillier by saying, "What is your name?"

This is a fatal mistake, for everybody believes his name does it, says it, proves it, and very definitely justifies the intrusion.

"Arthur Wilmanforthantenna."

Well, there's no such name, or at any rate no such name as the name Sherwood Anderson believed he *heard* the man say, and so in straightening out that little complication the visitor without a gift begins to tell Sherwood Anderson his exciting adventures as an unpublished writer of twenty-two years, with twenty-two rejected novels, and then he says, "What am I doing wrong?"

Robert Benchley would have said, "Writing. Give it up. Now, go home and thank God you are an American."

Visitors are, in short, a very special order of creature, whether from outer space or the eighth house down the street, which is the house in which several thousand visitors at my door have stated that they live.

The actual house is white stucco and a retired old man named

John lives in it with his faithful wife whose name is Jane: he worked for forty-two years as a clerk at PG&E, and he met Jane on the job and took her away from the excitement of the job forty-one years ago. Pacific Gas and Electric, in case you don't know. The pilot lights alone consume a couple of million dollars worth of energy every year in a medium-sized town, but unlike the sensible French hardware no American piece of hardware connected to any order of automatic supply of energy has a valve that can be conveniently shut. But then this is not about the bogus energy crisis, it is about visitors, so I can mention the two former students at the Actors Studio who quickly said—yes, precisely—"Hi, we just got here in that car across the street, from Brooklyn, we made it in only six days and six nights, we want to produce *The Cave Dwellers*. Did you get our letters, we sent sixteen?"

Well, of course I did get their letters, and so remembering the example of Robert Benchley I said, "I don't want you to produce *The Cave Dwellers*. I am opposed to the Actors Studio. You surely didn't drive 3,000 miles to stop at this door, you have relatives in Hollywood, or a campaign to revolutionize the movie business, so get along to those matters, while I get back to my work—yes, I work here, right here in this tract house, where I live."

The second visitor said, "Lou, tell him your interpretation."

Lou quickly said, "You know the old man called the King in the play, and the old woman called the Queen, I want them to be one person."

They teach you to think at the Actors Studio, you see, and Lee Strasberg and Elia Kazan just don't like people wanting to get into the theater not to think.

"Go on down to Hollywood, please," I replied and shut the door.

Thirty years ago, out of something like a kind heart, I permitted two Actors Studio students to produce *Hello Out There*, at an off-Broadway theater, and I myself went to the opening night, along with Brooks Atkinson, who in his review remarked that the play seemed unclear. Of course it was, the people in it were unclear and were performing to themselves not to the audience.

What I'm saying is, we really don't need visitors from outer space to astonish and even scare us half to death. the visitors from innerspace do just fine.

My instructions to everybody I know who is harassed by such visitors is this: Tell them quickly, "Go home to your father, and your mother. They are your people, they know you, and I don't, and don't want to, because I've got my own father and mother, and also my own son and daughter, and that's all I can manage."

Still, there will be visitors, as we all know, don't we? And now and then we will weaken out of simple boredom and say, "Ah, come on in and tell me your story, I'm sure it is *heroic*."

HILDEGARDE FLANNER

HILDEGARDE FLANNER is a California literary treasure. Her fame is not wide, but is precious to those who are acquainted with her sensitive renderings of her personal landscape. Her ways were as gentle as her lyrics; her love of the land passionate and strong.

Lisa Connolly, a freelance writer, interviewed her for us in 1977. Flanner was living in Calistoga with her architect husband, Frederick Monhoff. Attuned to this California valley, she reflected its beauty and its violation in her writings. Poems came to her, she said, when she was ready for them. "Ideas are like sparks that occur when two wires touch."

After this interview was published (December, 1977) accompanied by several of her poems, we approached Flanner for more of her work. She wrote to us in February, 1978.

I am sending you a few pages for consideration that might lead to something else. I have a series of diaries dating from 1929. Heavens!

Enclosed is a sample. It is a memory of how I took my mother to Yosemite, trying to avoid anything higher than a mole-hill as she could not abide heights. I have records of wonderful spring wildflower events as of 1931, a trip to Morongo Indians Reservation to witness various ceremonies, and so on.

I bought the Yosemite piece, which had a balance of humor and local history, and asked to see what she had on the Morongo Indians.

In March, 1978, she replied:

> I find three visits in the back country to Indian ceremonials, all of considerable interest. I think: The Burial of the Head Feather; The Burning of the Clothes; The Burning of the Images. Plus personal comments, details, and goings-on. My husband, Frederick Monhoff, made etchings, one of each ceremony which really show detail better than a photo, I believe. I will get these sent off to you as soon as I can manage. . . .

We published the Morongo Indian article with Monhoff's etchings. By that time he had died, and she was deeply wounded but seemed to draw solace from the land and her memories.

We asked her for poetry.

She sent some. She also sent a beautiful essay about a huge, old cherry tree that had been on her farm forever and finally had to be cut down because it was dying. As it fell, Hildegarde took her grandson to inspect the tree and discovered a live, creature-world still finding shelter in the aged roots—a continuity of life beneath the surface.

I sent my praises. Because I was leaving the magazine, it was the last piece of hers that I published—"The Last Bough," November, 1980. She replied:

> I prize your comments on "The Last Bough" and thank you with all my heart and spirit. Alas, that our association is ended. . . . I shall cling to a relationship that is now dear to me. . . . Devotedly.

We kept up an occasional correspondence until she died in 1987. A collection of her work called *Brief Cherishing* includes "The Last Bough," but here I share her California poetry.

HILDEGARDE FLANNER

Poems by Hildegarde Flanner

■ HILLS OF SAN SIMEON

The unearthly hills of San Simeon
Rise before me like moons displaced,
Pellucid, commingling how many times,
O cycling domes, O amber-spaced.

Not nostalgia, never my home,
Why should these hills, like worlds of light,
(Seen but once and glimmering then)
Float smooth and ravishing up my sight?

I must go back to them, I shall with slipping
Feet on the slick grass, and burning hand,
Climb the great slopes of this enchantment
And stare down the vision in rock and in sand.

■ VINTAGE (NAPA VALLEY)

My neighbor, the vintner, has an old stone wall
And over it eases in dark loose green
An ivy, elated with crimson each fall

As if, in a valley whose honour is wine,
Whose fields are ritual to the last grape,
Even the ivy, the visionless vine

Is whipped by a dream that cries in the stone,
Yield from the richness of your want
Till in winey nimbus of its own,

In winefall of colour over the wall
The dry stem is fluid with coral and rose
And the first crush and most ruby of those.

I brighten my eye, I hold out my glass,
Poor in spirit, poor in thirst,
And still get more than my right of grace

For if no grape hangs upon the vine
Yet sugars of excitement swell
In craze of vintage beyond belief

And intensity pours
from a falling leaf.

■ TIN CANS AT KEELER (OWENS DRY LAKE)

Here in the desert is a pallid lake
That once was murmurous upon its bed
With sparkle lapping on the inland shore.
Now all the lolling waves are pulverdead
And not a single water rears its head
And no blue brook with shiver of great drops
Comes this far boiling keenly on the land.
Man stole the water and the stricken lake
Lies like a trance and staring in the sand.
No flash nor spread of wave, no wet shimmer.
Just one thing shines here under the bare skies—
A heap of cans, new-dumped. The enormous glitter
Beats in the air and quivers where it lies,
And the brood of dirty brightness multiplies.

■ JANUARY ORCHARD

A state of light on winter boughs,
A hover of lilac on the tree,
A grove asleep in amethyst,
Drive terror from mortality.

If dying could be done like this,
A dreaming upright for a spell,
While inner secrets are awake
Planning enormous miracle,

If death were done like orchards,
Flower folded, never lost,
It would be worth the anguish,
It would be worth the frost.

■ THE OLD ROCKING CHAIR AT LILAC

As we went through the town of Lilac,
The tiny town of Lilac, fifty years ago,
We passed a house, and on the porch
There sat an empty rocking chair
Amiably rocking to and fro.
It hummed and rocked and watched the path
Spin under the spinning feet of the quail
Away into the azure brush,
And it watched the black flycatcher blink
His silky wing in the hot sky,
And it watched a young man and woman
Watching an old chair rock as we went by.

Hello, old chair, you knew we would return some day.
You and I will sit a spell alone;
Rock, old chair, be glad and rock,
Put your strong arms around me,

158

You know someone is coming soon,
You know someone is almost here.

Rock hard, old chair,
Rock to the ends of the chaparral,
Rock all over the top of the hill,
God help you, rock for joy until you crack,
Tell the great town of Lilac, tell the tiny world,
We shall all go into the past
And through the mountains.

But the road comes rocking back.

■ LAKE MONO FROM THE AIR

You! After half a century once more You!
Seen in commemorative light as though
I caught you looking at yourself
Full of night's small stars and dawn's big planets.
Huzza down there! I see your craters rise,
The black one and the white,
Old mystics whose fossil fires excite
Me strangely now as when, such a young thing,
I saw you first and knew by the ringing
Of my bones there must be two dominions,
The black light and the white,
And could not say which angel finished me.

Mono, to-day I am eerie and left over
From long ago, I glide above you
In terrible elegance of speed
And cannot hope to return, by foot or heaven,
But suddenly see you whole with quickening eyes
in love and astonishment not ever given
To the slow, soft clutter of a girl's surprise.

159

Vaya con Dios
Dan Dutton

LARRY L. MEYER & DAVIS DUTTON

DAVIS DUTTON &
LARRY L. MEYER

T O WRITE OF Davis Dutton and Larry Meyer makes me
smile even as I remember. They were the editors of *Westways* who hired me. Thrust into their midst, it was immediately
clear that this would be a lively experience. The editorial staff (we
were five) worked in one large, book-lined room. We each had a
space, but the cross-talk and openly expressed opinions bounced
through the air, eliminating areas of rank and privacy. Yet Meyer
and Dutton were respected and in charge. There were opinion
differences but none that were beyond solution.

Both Meyer and Dutton came out of the UCLA Journalism
School. There the similarity ended, though their compatibility was
a constant. Meyer, a big bombastic fellow, was given to extremes
of high and low. He loved literature and sports. In the spring he
often came to work aching from too much baseball and smelling of
ointment to relieve his tired muscles. Dutton, lesser in size only,
was a genial man who loved small jokes and tall tales that belied
his vast knowledge of California history, music, and art. He had in
fact produced *A California Portfolio*, which tells the story of the
State in "words and pictures"—a lucid, valuable chronology.

They set a mood that was relaxed and productive. We could whistle while we worked and still meet a deadline. When days wore thin, one or the other would step up to the dictionary stand, use it as a lectern, and orate on any given subject with comic profundity. Dutton, an adept mimic, recited Chaucer in euphonious style. Meyer was prone to quote from e.e. cummings, T.S. Eliot, or Yates. There were few restraints. When they left the magazines for a new venture, we partied, but not happily.

I could not fill their shoes—my feet were not that big. I had to design my own last and hope that the sole would tread well. We kept our friendship alive through the years. Meyer became a journalism professor at Long Beach State and has written books from history to fathering. Dutton [with wife Judy and brother Doug] owns the most browseable, eclectic bookstores in Los Angeles (new and used), filled to overflowing. No chain store mentality. Dutton has a real acquaintance with the books he harbors.

So it was that in planning a bicentennial issue for July 1976, I thought of Dutton and Meyer as the most likely duo to create a correspondence between Father Serra and Thomas Jefferson that would inform the East about the West—that vast unknown territory. What kind of colonization was going on there? Jefferson might indeed have been interested in what lay beyond the Eastern revolutionary site. Dutton and Meyer seized on the idea. Meyer would take responsibility for Jefferson and Dutton for Father Serra. They composed an exchange so authentic in style that when it was published many of our readers believed the letters to be actual and we chuckled at the reaction. A hoax is a hoax. This was our first and only piece of fiction.

What if such an exchange had actually taken place? The letters might have found a haven in the archives instead of being unearthed in a garage sale, as the authors claimed.

Check them out, if you will.

■

Jefferson/Serra Correspondence

BY LARRY L. MEYER AND DAVIS DUTTON

A small bundle of letters, discovered on April 1, 1976, at a Pico-Rivera garage sale, points to an early contact between that industrious founder of California's missions, Father Junipero Serra, and the illustrious protestant polymath Thomas Jefferson. It is admittedly hard to believe that this unlikely pair could have found the time and the means to communicate from opposite ends of a still largely wild continent. Yet stranger things have happened. We make no claim for the authenticity of that which follows but it would be a dereliction of journalistic duty to withhold these letters from public scrutiny.

AUGUST 12, 1777

Dear Fra. Junipero Serra,

I have fervent hopes that this letter may reach you, and find you in that degree of health necessary to the performance of your considerable duties. Only recently did I learn of the Spanish occupation of Alta California, and your office of Father of Missions, in accordance with the wishes of your king, Carlos III.

As must be known to you, we are presently at war to secure our liberty from our own king, George III of England, who means to return the yoke on us for the pleasure of England's merchants. The conflict, I must concede, is not running in our favor, suffering being commonplace among our citizens. War is always lamentable, yet in this case, necessary.

Hostilities have not extinguished the more laudable side of man, which is the restless expansion of his knowledge. Therefore I am moved by curiosity to ask you about California, and whatever you may know of other lands to our west, and to your east.

Our ignorance is vast, and I would be indebted to you for whatever information you could send. Drake reported Indians on that coast. Have you met with many? What trees, plants and foodstuffs grow there? What mines are operating? Is the climate subhumid and the visibility most clear, as is said of all lands west of the great river Mississippi? Many tales have been told here of those strange and boundless lands, among them the sightings of unicorns, griffins, elephants and leopards. My investigations tell me that this cannot be true, the former being inventions of the superstitious, the latter being beasts found only in the torrid belt. Likewise circulating are stories of a lake of gold and a mountain of silver. I discount them entirely; Nature is too wise to engender such monstrosities.

I doubt not the French, lately interposed between our peoples, have been in some measure responsible, as it is their habit to exaggerate whatever it pleases them to discover. Of more worthy attention, I think, is the Northwest Passage, or Strait of Anian, which has been sought by Europe's mariners for more than 200 years. Maps that include this feature position it just to the north of you, above California, where it is said to facilitate an easy ship passage to the riches of Cathay. Do you know anything of it? My colleague, Mr. Benjamin Franklin, has read an article describing a sailing through this coveted waterway in the year 1640 by a countryman of yours, Admiral Bartholomew de Fonte of Peru. Do you know the particulars of his adventure? Our intelligence informs us that the illustrious Captain James Cook sailed from England aboard *Resolution* the year last to rediscover this prized strait. Have you seen anything of him? By my calculation, Cook should be putting into your coast ere long.

You would ever be in receipt of my gratitude for enlightening me on California and the western extremities of this continent. And tell me everything about yourself, because all will be interesting to me. What are your amusements, literary and social?

I am with great and sincere attachment, dear sir, your affectionate admirer and servant.

Thos. Jefferson

To Thomas Jefferson
Monterey, Alta California
22 September 1778

Dear honored Sir,

It was a pleasure to receive yours of 8.12.77. The letter, Sir, confirms your reputation as a man of considerable knowledge and understanding. I am honored that you should favor me with your inquiries.

Let me first offer my hopes for a speedy resolution of the current conflict on the Atlantic Seaboard. Once your independence is achieved, I can only pray that Concord will thenceforth reign o'er North America, and that together we may work toward a state of friendly and mutually profitable intercourse.

We began our labors here in 1769, but found this place to be anything but that El Dorado told of by the early scribes. We discovered neither riches, nor Amazons when we arrived, though on our first march up country I half-expected to see such wonders, so often had I heard these falsehoods bandied on the lips of our lusty leather-jackets. [A term for the Spanish-American foot soldier who wore a thick, protective doublet of cowhide.] What greeted us, instead, was a wretched lot of heathens, dwelling in ignorance of the True Faith and the blessings of Civilization.

Into this outpost of Infidels our little band has come, bearing both Cross and Sword, the former to guide them, the latter to goad them.

By rough calculation, there may be upwards of 100,000 Indians dwelling in the whole of Alta California. With the larger number of these savages we have, as yet, had no contact. Yet, I will describe for you as completely as possible the diverse character and curious customs of these natives.

[The next page of the manuscript is missing. Serra, we can presume, here described the Indians' habits, trades, industries, recreations, diversions, foodstuffs, pharmacopoeia, crafts, costumes, villages and family life, beliefs, languages, as well as their physical appearance, state of health, and manner in which they greeted the Spaniards on their arrival.]

Some of these savages merely shunned us, some feared us, while others acted in a thieving, insolent manner until they could be won over by gifts of glass beads and other trinkets. Some tribes immediately welcomed us into their midst, offering us food, fireside and friendship. I well remember one night during the summer of '69. Our party, short on rations and exhausted by the long day's march over rough terrain, stumbled into an Indian *rancheria* near Santa Barbara, a camp of perhaps 100 brush huts. The savages, after sharing with us a meal of mussels, seeds and oak-corn mush, did then begin to serenade us with flutes, rattles, and drum. Dancers, both men and women of a most immodest sort, joined the musicians, turning the night into one of *fiesta*. Finally, well after midnight, we were compelled to ask them to desist, for we wished to retire. Our entreaties had merely the effect of making them the more ardent in their caterwaulings. I myself, despite the pain in my leg, did rise and try to wave them off, but they misinterpreted this as a desire on my part to join the dance, and they did try to pull me by the cassock into their revels. We pled the more for peace, but to no avail. At last, we were forced to hurl stones into their midst to show our displeasure. Only then did they stop.

Modesty and morality, in the civilized sense, were scarcely known to these people. Licentiousness, I regret to say, abounds. Young people casually cohabitate without benefit of marriage and in cases of adultery the mere payment of 6 or 8 clam shells to the injured party is deemed sufficient to set things right. By this system a cuckold may prosper.

They are as casual with their possessions as with their wives. They have no locks at the doorways of their huts, yet thievery amongst them seems not a problem. They pay but little regard to sanitary precepts, and their *rancherias* are generally noisome, squalid places.

We have done our utmost to destroy these unsanitary enclaves and have removed many hundreds of Indians to the mission, where we are teaching them useful trades, the fundamentals of agriculture, and the rudiments of civilized, Christian comportment. Some have balked at these necessary disciplines. Others rebel at the restrictions upon their licentiousness, the destruction of their villages and their resettlement in mission compounds. Many do not understand why we must segregate men and women, boys and girls.

Despite the obstacles, we are making progress. I sometimes dream of a California a century or two hence, when the Indians of this place have been raised from the darkness and have taken their rightful place as full-fledged members of our European Civilization, transplanted to the shores of America. I remain, dear Sir, your faithful servant,

Junipero Serra, O.F.M.

Nov. 28, 1780

Dear Fra. Serra,

No pleasure can exceed that which I received from your letter of September, 1778. Great risks attend all correspondence that goes by sea, trebly so in times of war, and we must each rejoice at our triumph over all hazards. Now, Sir, I can call you ally as well as friend; for as word may have reached you, Spain, your nation and sponsor, has joined the war against tyrannical Great-Britain, hostilities commencing in the summer of 1779.

Your revelations on the California Indian are most welcome. As you describe them, given to revelry and of a passive disposition, they appear an exception to those on our side of the continent. Yet may I prevail upon you to provide me with further detailed observations?

As governor of Virginia, with British forces only recently invading the coastlands of our dominion, threatening the safety of our citizens, I have been sorely pressed in my duties. Notwithstanding these trials, I am busily employed preparing a book, at the request of the Frenchman Monsr. Marbois, acquainting him with the State of Virginia and what I know of the western parts of this fecund continent. My notes, imperfect and wanting more talent from the writer, touch upon subjects, say, of rivers, mountains, manufactures, productions mineral, vegetable and animal, religion, laws, government, aborigines. On this last point I still lack the information I would wish.

In my youth I had the advantage of observing Indians at my father's plantation. But now there are very few among us. This pleases most of my countrymen, including my colleague, Mr. Franklin, who has remarked that the free distribution of strong spirits among them may be the appointed means of ridding ourselves of these obstacles to our agriculturists, who are moving west. With this I am in disappointment. I must also quarrel with the Paris philosophers who, without having seen an Indian, believe themselves qualified to describe him as a brute animal, less strong in body than Europeans, without ardor for his females, timid and cowardly, lacking in vivacity and the activity of mind.

It is my opinion that we could all learn from the French of the Mississippi River region in this regard. For more than a century their traders and coureurs de bois have lived amicably for the savages there. Mutual profit must be a motive for this harmony. Yet I maintain it is more than that. The French vagabonds appear more humane in general; respect more the qualities of the wilderness hunter who dwells within the rhythms of Nature; and are more tolerant of the differences between their societies. This is indeed supported by the readiness with which they take squaws.

My regret is that my fellow patriots have not followed the example of these unlettered fur men. The penalty has been tolerably high. Witness our recent troubles with Chief Pontiac. And now how most of the tribes have aligned themselves with the English in our Northwest, with the consequent and continued ravaging of our settlements in the Ohio Valley. (This river, favored by gentle currents and a smooth bosom, is surely the most beautiful on earth.)

The present conflict will one day end. As to that conclusion, I cannot guess what effect that will have on the aborigines. But I do lament that we have suffered so many of the Indian tribes to extinguish without our having collected and deposited in the records of literature their traditions, laws, customs, languages and other circumstances which might lead to a discovery of their relation to one another, or descent from other nations, which, I believe, were originally placed in Eastern Asia.

Now you see the course of my investigations. And why I am so persistent in inquiring after your discoveries in California, whence many wonderful anomalies have issued in the past, to the fascination of scientists everywhere. Please, Sir, tell me more of life in your parts? What diversions season your worthy labors? And what of your mountains, known as the Sierra Nevada on old maps? Stories that reach us here claim the summits are high. Yet I doubt they can compare with ours of the Blue Ridge. From data which many found a reasonable conjecture, we suppose the highest peak to be about 4,000 feet above the level of the sea.

I am entrusting to a vessel one hogshead of tobacco, the produce of the uncommon fertility of our soil. Doctor Walker, a friend of my father's, who was accustomed to visiting us at the Shadwell plantation in years past, believed the smoking of this luxuriant weed injurious to health. Yet I have not heard this contention proved. Therefore, accept with this gift of Virginia gold my assurances of high consideration and affectionate esteem.

Thos. Jefferson

16 March, 1781

Dearest Jefferson,

Yours of the 28th November, 1780, has just reached me, and its arrival has gladdened my heart.

We rejoice that our most Catholic Majesty, Charles III, has seen fit to join in the war upon England and that we are now allies, both in spirit and in arms.

Acknowledging this bond, we here in far-off California have lately raised a subscription for the support of your armies. Nearly 3,000 pesos have thus far been collected, and more is on the way. It is gratifying to see how our people have thrown themselves into the effort. Some examples:

Item. In San Jose, a parchment drive at the mission school netted nearly 300 pesos.

Item. A fund raising concert by the San Gabriel Hornblowers brought in 174 pesos.

Item. Saturday last the youngsters at Santa Ines held a community cart wash, while the ladies of the parish served a split-pea luncheon. Total 72 pesos.

Item. Here in Monterey a group of enterprising neophytes have been painting house numbers on the doorsteps and curbstones of every hacienda in the district. Thus far 50 pesos have been collected.

Now, as to the proposition put forth by those Parisian philosophers that the Indian is but a brute animal. Nothing could be more absurd. With my own eyes, I see these former savages who have accepted our Christian way of life rapidly raising themselves to the level which we call Civilization. They are skilled artisans, accomplished musicians and good Christians. And if further proof is needed, let me point out that Pope Paul, in a Bull of 1537, has already declared that the Indians of the Americas are *Rational Beings.* To my knowledge, there has been no such pronouncement regarding the philosophers of France.

A delegation of Indians from the Santa Barbara mission arrived here last month with an astonishing revelation. It seems they have found an innovative use for the black tarry substance that oozes from the fissures and faults along the coast. By mixing this substance (which they call ooze-fault) with crushed gravel, they have devised a material which can be applied to the ground as a sort of pavement upon which men, animals and vehicles can travel. They have petitioned me for a contract to apply the substance to sections of El Camino Real. I gave the scheme my whole-hearted blessing and the results thus far are highly encouraging.

Think of it, Jefferson, a broad, smooth band of ooze-fault stretching from San Diego, to San Francisco and beyond—the speed, the ease, the economy of travel on such a road. The journey between San Francisco and San Diego could be reduced to as little as six days on such a thoroughfare.

This road would have neither tollgates nor impediments and would therefore be, as Brother Desideratus jestingly remarked after vespers the other evening, a free-way. I rather like the sound of the word.

If our trial applications here in Monterey prove correct, then we shall begin immediately to lay ooze-fault all along the route. The work (Mr. Hamilton should find this of interest) shall be paid for not out of the Pious Fund, but rather by the imposition of a grass tax levied on all horses and mules which travel the road.

Governor de Neve suggested that we also impose a tax on shoe leather, since many pedestrians will use and benefit from this ooze-fault free-way, but my colleague Fra Crespi (an ardent walker and arch-conservative in matters fiscal) remonstrated thusly: "But Governor, would you tax men's soles?" De Neve relented, but he has power and is not one whose toes should be carelessly stepped on. I should not like to be in Crespi's sandals right now.

Father Bonaventura writes me from Southern California saying that the Indians residing in the new Pueblo de Los Angeles are developing into a remarkable company of actors and entertainers. He not altogether jokingly predicts that L.A. [This is the first recorded use of the now commonly accepted abbreviation.] will soon be known as the entertainment pueblo of the world.

The attendant notoriety has, of course, occasioned a few problems. Young people from elsewhere, dreaming of theatrical careers, flock to the pueblo, only to find disappointment. Some become busboys and waitresses at the Olvera St. cafés. Others congregate in front of the Plaza Pharmacia, hoping for bit parts as cowherders or milkmaids. The existence of these frequently unruly drug-store *vaqueros*, as they have become known, has thrown an additional burden on the limited law enforcement resources of the pueblo.

The most popular of the current plays is entitled *Los Dos Hermanos*. It is a story concerning two brothers who are born, as we say, on the other side of the arroyo. They are both lovingly raised by their widowed mother. One of the brothers decides to enter the priesthood, but the other one takes the wrong path, and

becomes a bandito. The story ends as the bad brother is appre-
hended robbing the poor box at the very church where the good
brother is the Priest. The bad brother is sentenced to be hanged and
the good brother, despite the many wrongs done to him comes to
the gallows to administer the *Sacramentas.* The magistrate, moved
at this display of filial devotion, commutes the sentence and
remands the bad brother to the custody of the good. The entire cast
sings a song at the end, and this is followed by a humorous sketch
done by the sensational comedy team of Cisco and Pancho. It is all
very wholesome with some good lessons, I think. [Records indicate
the first performances of *Los Dos Hermanos* took place May 20,
1782 at the old Teatro Million Dollar.]

The director of the play is Father Histrionicus, whom Crespi
considers one of the few real showmen in the business. "Hist," as
his friends in the industry call him, was recently honored by his
colleagues at the Friar's Club and presented with a small gold
likeness of Saint Oscar. I had the pleasure of attending the ceremony and was impressed by his acceptance speech in which he
modestly, and a little tearfully, thanked "all those people who had
made this moment possible." He then lashed out at the immortal-
ity of some of our writers and producers, specifically citing the
recently suppressed *Last Fandango in Chichicastenango* as a "new
low in dramatic filth."

But enough of this for now. I must retire early. Tomorrow
morning we leave for San Juan Capistrano to greet the swallows on
their return. I am, and remain, your friend and servant,

Junipero

July 4, 1783

Dear Sir,

I received days ago your favor of March 16, 1781, and was
happy to find your civilizing enterprise meeting with success. What
you tell me of life in California is most engaging and in some
particulars astonishing. I am very curious about this black ooze-

fault with which you cover your mission trace. I would suppose this substance to be akin to what we sometimes call pitch tar, and believe that were we to have it here we could well apply it to our own roads, which during our temperate seasons oft become quagmires. But does your ooze-fault resist your heavy spring and summer rains? If so, we could well look to its importation. From what I have read, this pitch tar can be useful when it approaches the condition of a solid. But if it is in too liquefied a state, I do not foresee it ever serving any human purpose.

I was most surprised to learn of the high development of the theatrical art in California. You do eclipse us here. As mostly planters of the earth, we neglect the gayer muses, yet escaping also the meaner vices accompanying such exhibitions, as are found in Paris and London. I should note one exception to the above. That is New York, the one in the thirteen former colonies where such extravagances and caperings are a delight to its inhabitants, who fancy themselves the most sophisticated of New World beings, and boast about their public entertainments. Here Mr. Hamilton and his banker friends prosper among those who have clustered themselves in the unsanitary confines of their island city. It should also be said that New York is a breeding ground of loyalist sentiment and those who would be kingmakers. Alas, should the present conflict be resolved in our favor, the arrogance and profligacy of New York may yet prove the undoing of our republic. This disagreeable neighbor may well lead us all to ruin and the court of bankruptcy.

You, personally, Sir, are due from us our deepest gratitude. Your diligent collection of funds from the California missions has materially contributed to our triumph and is surely a most demonstrable expression of your own republican sympathies.

The westward extension of our lands determines that we shall soon be neighbors. This, I have been informed, distresses your representative in France, the Count Aranda, who foresees friction between our peoples along the broad Mississippi and the violation by Americans of His Most Catholic Majesty's territory. Let me assure you that Spain has no cause for worry on that account from this Republic. The treaty of peace will provide us with land enough to provide many times our present numbers with fields to sow; even more earth to plant would only thin and scatter our population at a dangerous time. Moreover, cultivators of the earth are the most virtuous and peaceful of citizens, recognizing as kings, generals and bankers do not that war is ever wasteful and destructive of man's nobler instincts.

Yet a single cloud does hover above our shared horizon. It is the rumor that your government is about to close the Port of New Orleans to our river commerce. I must conclude that this is only the casual gossip of indolent bureaucrats with no greater mischief to make. Otherwise, violent events would attend any such constriction of this vital trade for our western farmers, who have reputations for possessing long rifles and short tempers.

Spain and our infant confederacy must not neglect our communion of interests. We here could wish no better neighbor on our border than your nation. France, though we have looked upon her as our natural friend, has an impetuosity of temper, an energy and restlessness of character which is best appreciated from a distance, say an ocean's width. As for England, I fear they will not take the loss of their colonies easily; and that from their stronghold in Canada will inflict upon us only ill. My idea, then, is to urge a number of my countrymen to learn the Spanish language, with a mind to our future peaceful connections, and forgetting not that the ancient history of America is written in that language.

But these are public matters for nations to entertain. What of you, dear friend? How is your health? Robust, I trust. Write to me and be assured of the interest I take in your success, as well as the warmth of those sentiments of attachment with which I am your affectionate servant.

Hasta la vista

Thos. Jefferson

Dearest Tomaso,

Yours of July 4 last has arrived, and I am heartened to learn of your successes, both on the field of battle and at the negotiating table. I feel encouraged in the knowledge that we shall be neighbors, though I do, in candor, harbor certain fears over the future of the North American Continent. Can four powerful governments—yours, the French, the English, and our own—learn to live in peace? Just now this vast land seems large enough for each of us to pursue our separate objectives, but the continent is growing smaller. Already your people are spilling over your Cumberland and Appalachian Mountains, into that great *llano* known as the Valley of the Mississippi. Will your restless, energetic people be satisfied to stop there, or will they want, as we say, the whole enchilada?

But tell me, Tomaso, how do you call your new country? Is it to be a kingdom, a confederation or a republic? And who is to be your ruler? Will General Washington now become King? Or do others—even yourself—covet the hereditary title? Ah, there is so much I yearn to know, and I am growing old. Will your established church be that of the English Episcopacy, or will you, as rumoured, opt for some Calvinist persuasion? I know we Catholics stand but little chance of being considered for the job, yet I enclose several pamphlets lately printed in Rome in an effort to convince you of our merits. Now for some news of California.

We are experiencing growing pains: the puebloization of California has put many strains on us and created many problems. On my recent trip to Los Angeles I was shocked to see the number of cantinas that have popped up around the Plaza. Young people on balmy nights (even on the Sabbath) stroll up and down Olvera Street or loiter at the taco stands, casting flirtatious glances at one another (and doing what else, God only knows).

By the by, I promised the Alcalde that I would see if Dr. Franklin had any thoughts on the dissipation of the smoke and fumes that collect over Los Angeles. On certain days the atmosphere is oppressive. Stern remedies are called for.

And yet, to compel Señor Reynaldo to shut down his forge, or require Mama Vasquez (whose great stove belches forth from early morning to late at night) to close her cantina would impose hardships on all. A prohibition on the burning of brush, litter and cow chips has been considered, but it is thought the people might rebel at these measures, and already there is enough discontent abroad in the land.

Crespi and I thank you for the tobacco. Keeping a pouch or two for ourselves, we have distributed the rest among the Indians and soldiers. All agree it has a smooth, mild taste, and Dr. Pedro Prat, our chief physician, declares it to contain 15 percent less tar and nicotine than the leading local brand.

Alas, Tomaso, the hour is late and I am tired. My prayers go with you and yours. May peace and tranquility reign over our land *in perpetuem*. Write soon and *vaya con Dios*.

Junipero

Postscript

THE BOOK ENDS HERE, not because that's all there is, but because it's all I intended—to set down a few personal thoughts about the editor-writer relationship; to show how such compatibility that brings out the best in each can be an exhilarating exchange. At least, so it has been for me. As I close, an incident comes to mind that dramatizes the high reward of such an exchange. It has to do with Ariel Durant, who collaborated with her husband William on eleven volumes of *The Story of Civilization*.

Ariel Durant died in 1981 at age eighty-three. A good age and a full life. Yet I was affected. What a feisty woman she was, and how passionate about her "William" and their work.

I had only one brief meeting with her, in 1975 after some phone conversations, but she is fixed in my memory. I had written to ask if she would agree to be interviewed for a series we were running on women who were leaving their imprint on our time. Would she let me know how she felt about participating?

Two weeks later, I was at my desk on a Friday afternoon. There was a phone call. "This is Ariel Durant," she announced in a raspy, New York-accented voice. She had received my letter and *did not* want to be interviewed. Reporters always misquoted her.

She wanted to be left alone. She didn't have time to waste. She and Will were being honored for *The Age of Napoleon*, which required much travel. They would be away for a good while.

I quickly recovered from her barrage of negatives and sympathized with her reluctance to subject herself to misquotes, but assured her that our writer, Robert Bryan, was a sensitive interviewer. He had done a fine study of ceramic artist Beatrice Wood. If she should decide to reconsider and talk to Bryan, we would show her the article before publication, something we rarely did, so she could approve it. There was a moment of silence. I sensed I had her attention; at least she did not hang up. She asked me to write her another note after she returned from the East. Then she would decide. It took months of patient negotiating before she agreed.

Bryan wrote a perceptive, charming piece about Ariel, nee Ida Kaufman, who at age fifteen, married her professor Will Durant. She was a lively spirit even though they "lived, ate, and slept history." Theirs was a strict regimen. "He's a monk and I'm a nun," she said. Asked about a possible biography, she answered, "When I'm in my coffin, with one leg sticking out . . . I'll tell the truth, pull my leg in and bang the lid down . . . and then they can publish my biography."

I sent her the finished script for approval. She wrote back,

> The Ms is excellent. I have made a few punctuation marks, subject to your consent; otherwise, no complaint.
>
> Yours, Ariel Durant

But we were not yet finished. I needed some photographs and phoned her again. "I've got plenty of pictures, but you'll have to come up here to see them."

I drove up the Hollywood Hills to their Spanish-style house. The familiar face of gentle Will Durant greeted me. I asked for Ariel and explained that I had an appointment with her to look through some photographs. She wasn't home, but he asked me to come in. She had gone somewhere with her sister. He suggested that I wait. She was sure to be back soon.

I followed him into the kitchen. The table was covered with open newspapers and a *New Yorker*. Would I mind if he finished an article he was reading while I waited? Of course not. I sat quietly and watched the man whose books on philosophy and history were published the world over. And here he was in an old-fashioned kitchen totally absorbed in a magazine article—a most prosaic scene. In a short while, Ariel arrived—a white-haired sprite dressed in black. "Did you forget that you had an appointment?" he asked her teasingly.

No she did not forget. She was here, wasn't she? Then this tiny lady commanded me, "Come," and I followed her through the disarray of the large living room to her cluttered desk. In case I noticed a bed in the living room, she explained, it was there because Will was having difficulty climbing the steps to the bedroom and was sleeping in his study. She had moved her bed down to be close to him in case he might need her during the night.

She sifted through piles of pictures, early snapshots—some with her daughter. Which could I have? "I can't give you those," she said brusquely. "You'll take them and they'll get lost. They are the only ones I have."

I promised to take special care. I would even have copies made at once and return the originals so she would have them back before publication. She would not budge. I tried another approach. "But you said if I came up I could select some pictures." She was quick to reply, "I said you could *look at* some pictures." We were at an impasse. I made one more try. "I have a transparency of a painting of you and Dr. Durant, but I need a couple of black and whites as well."

She put away the family pictures and brought out some professional publicity shots. "Maybe one of these." I chose one. She thought it made her look too old. I asked her to select two. She did. They were both of her and Will, glossy and flattering. "Thank you," I said, knowing enough to stop while I was ahead.

"You'll have to sign a paper for these. Write down how many pictures you have. Write that you'll return them." I wrote and signed.

She walked me to the door and spontaneously gave me a hug. I was surprised and touched. She might have been my very own tough, little mother who always said "no" before she said "yes." I started out, looked back toward the house. There, framed in a window, was Will; and there, in the doorway was Ariel—two intellectual giants, lifesize.

It's an image that will not go away. And why should it? In essence, that image and other fragments of memory are the bonus for a day's work that made it worth the effort.